MORE PAINTED LADIES

MODERN MILITARY AIRCRAFT NOSE-ART & UNUSUAL MARKINGS

RANDY WALKER

Schiffer Military/Aviation History
Atglen, PA

Acknowledgements

I am again indebted to a great many people for their invaluable assistance with this project:

Paul Bigelow
Jerry Knau
Roland Black
Vince Breslin
David F. Brown
Joe Bruch
Rich Curry
Chuck Denney
N. Donald
Bob Dorsey
Jim Dunn
Bob Esposito
Billie Faust
Rene Francillon
Jerry Fugere
Armon T. Gaddy, Jr.
Lynn Gasaway
Stanley D. Gohl
Mike Hill
Michael J. Hrivnak
Bob Johnston
Fran Johnstonbaugh

Cheryl Jones
Mark Lewis
Steve Link
Don Logan
Tammy Lulei
Jim Meehan
Dave Menard
Jim Moseley
Tracy M. Partelow
L. N. Paul
Robert V. Pease
Bobby Petty
John Phaler
Brian C. Rogers
Robert Root
Bob Shane
Robbie Shaw
M. D. Swann
Judith Szyszkowski
Dan Tasca
Wally Van Winkle
David M. Willford

Special thanks to "the Fox Crew":
Penney Bouse
Diane Canion
Jamie Lusk
Shari Taylor

And to my family for general encouragement and support.

Such a colorful and expansive subject is as difficult to exhaust as it is to cover definitively. I would enjoy hearing from anyone who has nose art stories, information or photos to share. A third volume is certainly not out of the question. Please feel free to contact me care of Schiffer Publishing.

Cover:
An especially fine painting by Gary Campbell graced the nose of KC-135E 58-0040, a 170th ARG, New Jersey ANG, tanker. Crew chief TSgt Scott Kellach took the name from the title of one of his favorite movies, liking the idea of EASY MONEY. The name of his daughter, Amber Lynn, appeared on the pouty beauty's name tag. Sadly this artwork, failing to meet the new "gender neutral" guidelines, was removed from the airplane.
Rene Francillon

Title page:
TIGERWOMAN II was F-4E 68-0346 from the 108th TFW, NJANG. The art nicely blended the 108th tiger mascot with the more traditional nose art fare. On 2 October 1991 this Phantom left McGuire AFB for her new home with the Turkish Air Force.
via Rene Francillon

KC-135A 63-8010, BAD BONES, is one example of the 93rd Bomb Wing's elaborate nose art. *93 BW/USAF*

Book Design by Bonnie Hensley

First Edition
Copyright © 1994 by Randy Walker.
Library of Congress Catalog Number: 93-84796

Printed in China.
ISBN: 0-88740-514-2

We are interested in hearing from authors with book ideas on related topics.

Opposite page:
Following the release of the Batman movie in 1989 "The Dark Knight" began turning up everywhere, including in nose art. BATMOBILE was a 93rd Bomb Wing KC-135A, 62-3497. *93 BW/USAF*

Published by Schiffer Publishing Ltd.
77 Lower Valley Road
Atglen, PA 19310
Please write for a free catalog.
This book may be purchased from the publisher.
Please include $2.95 postage.
Try your bookstore first.

CONTENTS

HIGH OCTANE, KC-135A 59-1522 belonged to the 93rd Bomb Wing at Castle AFB. Sadly, in keeping with current policy, much of the 93rd's fine artwork has been removed. *93 BW/USAF*

INTRODUCTION

Nose art, the practice of personalizing aircraft with names or artwork, has existed as a living and evolving art form since the earliest days of flight. The Second World War marked the golden age of nose art. New airplanes were produced in abundance and dispatched to all corners of the globe; crewed by a generation of young men with boundless imagination, whose desire for victory, home and female companionship – not always in that order – defined the genre as we know it today. In peacetime, nose art faded from the scene, to be revived over Korea, and to a lesser extent during the Vietnam War. The modern renaissance began in the mid-1980s with the FB-111s of the 509th Bomb Wing and the 380th Bomb Wing, and by the end of the decade, had spread throughout Strategic Air Command. Some of the finest artwork was produced by the Air Force Reserve and Air National Guard units, who in some cases had already been applying individualized markings to their aircraft on a limited basis for years. Though hard to measure, the positive effect of nose art on the morale and esprit de corps of the aircrews and maintenance personnel was evident. In 1991 nose art flew into harm's way with a new generation of fighting men and women, and continued to evolve. In the spirit of

KIMBERLY ANNE, A-10A 78-0603, was named after the wife of Capt. "Ty" Cobb, her pilot. Belonging to the 354 TFW, 355 TFS, she returned home to Myrtle Beach after completing 68 combat sorties, wearing kill markings for 2 radar sites, 12 artillery pieces, 12 tanks, 9 armored vehicles and 11 trucks destroyed. 354 TFW/USAF

World War II artwork that expressed contempt for the Axis leaders, Saddam Hussein proved to be a ready target for abuse in Persian Gulf War art. Bart Simpson and Batman appeared on F-16s and A-10s, just as Bugs Bunny and Daisy Mae decorated B-17s and B-26s almost fifty years before. As always, sexy pin-up girls remained a favorite subject. Active duty Tactical Air Command jets began sporting nose art, which had previously been forbidden; as did a handful of U.S. Navy and Marine aircraft.

Most of the Royal Air Force contingent, deployed as part of Operation Granby, also carried "warpaint" over new desert pink – ap-plied with an eye towards tradition and a very British sense of humor. Modern nose art had reached it's zenith. Now nose art is evolving again, to become "politically correct" in the 1990s. Subjects that some find offensive when painted on a bomber or tanker, such as the female form, will no longer be allowed on U.S. military aircraft. We shall see what effect, if any, this will have on the perpetuation of personal-ized markings; but certainly if the crews have a say in the matter, nose art will live on as it has in the past – changing when necessary, all but vanishing for years at a time, but always endur-ing.

CHAPTER I
B-1B LANCER

B-1B 86-0132 OH HARDLUCK now wears the new Gunship Gray scheme which follows the current trend towards gray airplanes. The first few aircraft repainted retain the 3-tone camoflauge colors on the nose radome – indicative of early problems with radar reflectivity in the new paint, which have since been eliminated. The nose art OH HARDLUCK originally carried has been faithfully reproduced with colors a bit more complimentary to the overall gray. With the dissolution of SAC, TAC, and MAC into ACC and AMC, Air Combat Command bombers and tankers acquired a "TAC-style" tail number application along with two-letter tail codes; such as "DY" for the 96th Wing aircraft based at Dyess AFB, Texas. *Walker*

B-1B 84-0055, 96 Wing, was named RIDGE RUNNER until 1991, when she was repainted in the new gray scheme. The name was then changed to "Sunrise Surprise" with Varga Girl artwork. *Jim Meehan*

B-1B 86-0131 ULTIMATE WARRIOR, previously "The 8th's Wonder", belongs to the 319th Wing. The photo was taken on 30 July 1992. *Don Logan*

CLASSY LADY is B-1B 85-0079, from the 28th Wing at Ellsworth AFB. Previously she was "Warrior's Dream", also with the 28th. *Don Logan*

B-1B 86-0121 MAIDEN AMERICA was one of two 319th Wing bombers (the other being 86-0111 "Ace In The Hole") utilized in setting new time-to-climb records in early 1992. The B-1B broke eight existing records at 215,000 and 225,000 pounds; and established four never before attempted records in the 335,000-pound weight class-including a climb to 40,000 feet in 9 minutes, 42 seconds. *Don Logan*

Shortly before the nose art was removed from all 319th Wing aircraft in 1992, B-1B 86-0118 IRON MISTRESS received this larger and more elaborate version of the artwork she carried for years. Of note is the warrior's shield, marked with the "sunflake"-half sun, half snowflake-also used for tail markings on 319th aircraft.
Don Logan

B-1B 83-0069, a 96th W aircraft, is named REBEL. This was one of the earlier examples of B-1B nose art.
Steve Link

This 384th Wing B-1B, 86-0124, is named WINGED THUNDER. The artwork – featuring bird of prey, lightning strike and triangle was chosen from entrants in a contest to design the first nose art for a McConnell B-1B. The triangle reflects the 384th Bomb Group's WWII B-17 tail markings, the letter "D" within a triangle, that was also applied to some 384th B-1's for a short time. *Walker*

SCREAMIN' DEMON is B-1B 85-0080, attached to the 384th Bomb Wing. *Walker*

Nose art on 319th Wing B-1B 86-0123 HIGH NOON gives one a look at the business end of an old west badman's gun. *Walker*

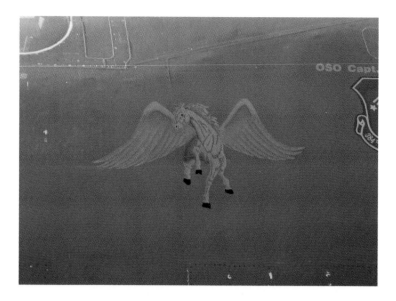

B-1B 86-0129, 384th W, was named PEGASUS years before the artwork was applied. *Walker*

Previously "Phantom" with the 28th BW, B-1B 86-0100 was renamed NIGHT HAWK by her 96th Wing crew chief. The 96th W's badge carries the motto: "e sempre hora" – it's always the hour. *Don Logan*

LOVELY LADY was B-1B 86-0103 of the 96th W. On 1 October 1993, the 96th Wing deactivated, with the 7th Wing – previously at Carswell – assuming control of B-1 operations at Dyess. *Don Logan*

BAD COMPANY was B-1B 86-0130 of the 384th Wing. The art was removed towards the end of summer 1992 along with the rest of the 384th's short-lived nose art. *Mark Lewis*

A patriotic bulldog, having broken free and going on the attack, is the subject of the artwork on B-1B 86-0135, THE WATCHDOG, 384th W. *Don Logan*

PEACE WARRIOR, B-1B 86-0140, is a 384th W aircraft. *Don Logan*

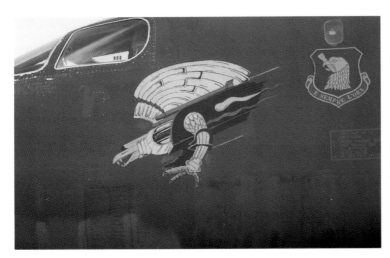

THE HELLION, B-1B 84-0057 belongs to the 96th Wing. Generally, nose art was carried on both sides of the 96th's bombers while B-1B's from other units – the 28th Wing, 319th Wing, and 384th Wing – featured art on the left side only. *Don Logan*

EXCALIBUR is B-1B 86-0122 from the 319th Wing at Grand Forks. Walker

Not "politically correct" or "gender neutral", this artwork appeared on B-1B 86-0134 WILD ASS RIDE of the 384th Bomb Wing. Walker

Reflecting the history of nose art within the 96th Wing the B-17G (44-85599) on static display at Dyess AFB was recently refurbished and painted to represent the WWII 96 BG's THE RELUCTANT DRAGON, 43-38133. The artwork was applied by Captain Matthew P. Glenn of the 337th BS. *Walker*

B-1B 83-0065 THE STAR OF ABILENE was the second Bone completed, and the first from a regular production block. This aricraft was named "Star Of Palmdale" at the factoy. The name was changed to reflect her assignment to the 96th BW and the first version of "The Star Of Abilene", with a B-1 silhouette inside a star, was applied.

The first B-1B, 82-001, also carried the "Star of Abilene" artwork while filling in at the delivery ceremonies at Dyess when -0065 was stuck at Offutt AFB with engine troubles. The second version of THE STAR OF ABILENE features a star swooping from west central Texas. Don Logan, Steve Link

CHAPTER 2
B-52 STRATOFORTRESS

Though the B-52Gs are fast becoming history, the B-52H will likely soldier on into the next century. B-52H 61-0017 REN-EGADE, a 92nd Wing BUFF, was photographed at Ellsworth AFB prior to her nose art being painted over; and had yet to receive the new tail code – "FC" for the Fairchild based aircraft. The marking below the name is the old 92nd Bombardment Group insignia, which consisted of a swooping Pterodactyl and the motto "Higher-Stronger-Faster." *Don Logan*

Traditional Varga Girl nose art, SAC TIME was carried by B-52G 59-2572, 93rd Bomb Wing. At least one other B-52G (58-0164, of the 416th Bomb Wing) was decorated with the same yawning beauty and the name "SAC TIME" – itself a play on words. *93 BW/USAF*

READY FOR DUTY, nose art on B-52H 60-0045 as of September 1988. One of Alberto Vargas' most popular pin-ups, this lady has been applied to countless aircraft since the original painting appeared in the April 1943 issue of Esquire magazine. *Jim Meehan*

B-52G 59-0183 VALKYRIE of the 93rd Bomb Wing was one of several BUFFS to receive the attention of artist Mark Cooke. The female warrior usually seen riding a giant polar bear is depicted here upon a leaping white war horse; grasping in one hand the Strategic Air Command emblem in the form of a shield, and in the other an olive branch and lightning bolts (also found in the SAC insignia). While most of her type will soon be scrapped, this B-52G is preserved at the Pima Air & Space Museum in Tucson, Arizona. *93 BW/USAF*

B-52G 58-0175 VIPER of the 379th Bomb Wing is seen at Jeddah on 2 March 1991 sporting 47 mission symbols. *Brian C. Rogers*

OLD CROW EXPRESS, B-52G 57-6492 from the 379th Bomb Wing at Wurtsmith AFB, Michigan, undertook 51 missions from the sprawling King Abdul Aziz International Airport at Jeddah, Saudi Arabia. *Brian C. Rogers*

RAGIN' RED, 416th BW B-52G 57-6501 carries 5 bomb symbols representing missions out of Moron, Spain. *Brian C. Rogers*

Surely one of the more frequent flyers assigned to the 1708th Bomb Wing (Provisional); B-52G 58-0203, named BLACK WIDOW by her 93rd BW crew chief, carries 55 white bombs for missions from Jeddah – with the half-century mark highlighted in red. *Brian C. Rogers*

Another 416th BW BUFF, B-52G 59-2583 RUSHIN' NIGHTMARE carries artwork created with the Cold War in mind; but with mission marks from an altogether different kind of war, showing five bombing sorties from Moron and 35 more from Jeddah. *Brian C. Rogers*

ALLEY OOP'S BOLD ASSAULT, B-52G 58-0159, 379 BW, had completed 24 bombing raids against targets in Iraq and Kuwait by 8 February 1991, with another 22 soon to follow. By the end of the year 58-0159 was retired from service. *Brian C. Rogers*

B-52G 57-6498 ACE IN THE HOLE, a 416th BW BUFF, deployed to RAF Fairford to become part of the 806th Bomb Wing (Provisional) during Operation Desert Storm. Fairford-based aircraft carried red mission tally bombs. The significance of the Iraqi flag is not clear. *Walker*

A good example of mission tallys of the type applied to the B-52's operated by the 4300th Bomb Wing (Provisional) from Diego Garcia during the Persian Gulf War. B-52G 58-0250 was a 42nd BW machine – as evidenced by the wing's insignia (aethera nobis or "With Us The Heavens") and "The Moose Is Loose" script which is found on most of the Loring aircraft. *Dan Tasca*

IRON MAIDEN is B-52G 58-0193 of the 416th BW, seen here at the London International Airshow in Ontario in June 1991. She carries 13 large black bomb symbols, indicating Gulf War service with the 801st BW (P) at Moron, Spain. *David F. Brown*

Here an unidentified crewman is seen adding another mission symbol to an otherwise very plain-appearing B-52G, 58-0216, upon her return to the island of Diego Garcia. This aircraft eventually completed 22 bombing sorties during the Gulf War. *42 BW via Dan Tasca*

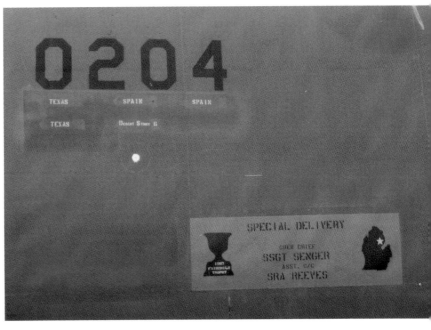

Aircraft have evolved immensely since the "Golden Age" of nose art – the Second World War; but the art form itself has changed little, and the symbols used by the crews to keep a running count of the missions they flew are virtually the same. Compare the art and mission symbols on TORCHY a Saipan-based 498th Bomb Group B-29 (42-24646) with those of Gulf War veteran B-52s. *AFM*

An unusual method of displaying B-52G 58-0204's Desert Storm mission count. Named SPECIAL DELIVERY, this 379th BW BUFF wears a subdued bomb silhouette – similar to those used to represent exercise deployments to locations such as Texas, Oklahoma or Spain – with the legend "Desert Storm 6" to denote 6 sorties flown out of Fairford. *Walker*

The insignia of the WWII 668th Bomb Squadron is carried on the right side of B-52H 60-0005, 416th Wing, 668th Bomb Group. *Jim Meehan*

SPECTER, a 93rd Bomb Wing B-52G (58-0199) was retired in June of 1991. This is one of many 93rd BW BUFFs to benefit from the attention of artist SSgt Mark Cooke. *Wally Van Winkle*

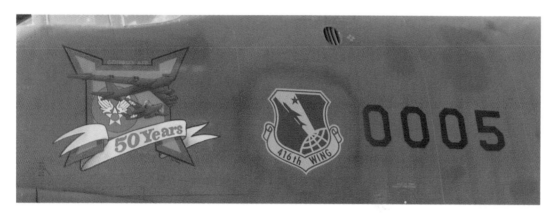

Art on the left side of 60-0005 commemorates the 50th Anniversary of the 416th Wing's home base, Griffiss AFB, activated 1 Feb 1942 near Rome, New York. *Jim Meehan*

This MONKEY BUSINESS artwork, featuring a decidedly unpleasant looking bomb-toting ape, immediately preceeded the Griffiss AFB 50th Anniversary markings on B-52H 60-0005. *Dan Tasca*

THE BLACK SWAN II was B-52G 57-6476. A 93rd Wing BUFF, she was named in honor of WWII B-17 42-29895 that served with the 91st Bomb Group. The artwork, featuring a fully-rigged sailing ship, was faithfully recreated on 57-6476. *93 BW/USAF*

B-52G 59-2584 was named MIDNIGHT EXPRESS during 1989. Taking an owl from the cover of an album by the rock group Rush, FLY BY NIGHT; Cooke incorporated the bomber (seen in a similar light) to create an effective and imaginative bit of nose art. *93 BW/USAF*

Another rendition of COMMAND DECISION, this time on B-52G 58-0221 of the 93rd Bomb Wing. The 93rd was SAC's first B-52 unit, formed in 1955 – shortly after the first "Command Decision" went to war in Korea. *93 BW/USAF*

THE LIBERATOR, 379 BW B-52G artwork, depicts an attacking eagle with a knife clutched in its beak, wearing a helmet and aiming a machine gun. *379 BW/USAF*

MIDNIGHT RENDEZVOUS was B-52G 59-2584 from the 93rd Bomb Wing. Another example of Mark Cooke's highly detailed and elaborate style, this piece drew inspiration from a segment of the motion picture Heavy Metal and the cover of the soundtrack album that featured very similar artwork. *93 BW/USAF*

WHAT'S UP DOC? is a B-52G, 58-0182, from the 379th Bomb Wing. The nose art is virtually identical to the unit emblem of the 579th Bomb Squadron, a WWII B-26 unit that served in Europe from 1943-46. *Bob Shane*

TREASURE HUNTER was B-52G 58-0168, 379th Bomb Wing. *L. N. Paul*

SWEET REVENGE, B-52G 59-2591 of the 379th Bomb Wing, was retired in June of 1992. Signed by artist "Vargo", the artwork shows Vulcan, the Roman god of fire and metalworking hammering out a lightning bolt. This design was apparently taken from the insignia of the 875th Bomb Squadron, a short-lived WWII B-29 outfit. *Wally Van Winkle*

This 410th BW B-52H, 60-0056, is named REAL STEEL. The large area of newer darker paint indicates a recent change of nose art. *Walker*

BLACK BUZZARD is another 379th Bomb Wing B-52G. *379 BW/USAF*

I'LL BE SEEING YOU, very traditional Vargas inspired nose art on B-52H 60-0024, 416th Wing in June 1992. *N. Donald*

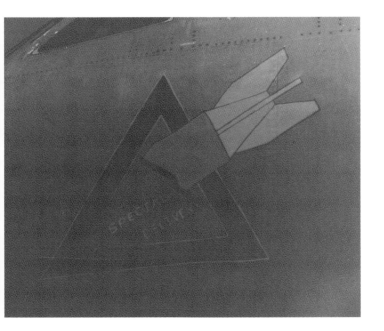

B-52G 58-0207 SPECIAL DELIVERY belonged to the 93rd Bomb Wing at Castle AFB in 1990 when this photo was taken. *93 BW/USAF*

SLIGHTLY DANGEROUS, B-52H 60-0034, belonged to the 410th Bomb Wing at K. I. Sawyer AFB. *Walker*

B-52G 59-2577, of the 93rd Bomb Wing, carries this aptly named artwork MAJESTIC. *93 BW/USAF*

B-52G 58-0165 ROLLING THUNDER, from the 416th Bomb Wing, captured on film while undergoing Program Depot Maintenance after returning home from Desert Storm. Mission marks claim 24 bombing sorties from Moron. *Walker*

Close-up view of the nose art on ROLLING THUNDER shows good details in the relatively small artwork. Note the bomber's mission symbols had been removed by the time she retired in 1992. *Bob Shane*

Inspired by artwork found on a WWII 8th Air Force B-17, TANTALIZING TAKEOFF is B-52G 57-6471 from the 97th Wing at Eaker AFB. She was flown to AMARC on 29 July 1992, and will eventually be scrapped there in accordance with the START treaty. *Bob Shane*

Named after a WWII-vintage 91st BG B-17F (42-29815) B-52G 57-6475 MIAMI CLIPPER last served with the 2nd Wing. She made her final flight on 20 Aug 1991. *Walker*

Seen at AMARC, with a protective coat of Spraylat covering the entire nose, BUFFASAURUS is B-52G 58-0194. *Bob Shane*

HOOSIER HOT SHOT is B-52G 57-6487, last operated by the 97th Bomb Wing at Eaker AFB. Inspired by the work of Vargas, this art and the name HOOSIER HOT SHOT first came together on 91st Bomb Group B-17G 42-38006. *Wally Van Winkle*

MISSBEHAVIN", artwork on B-52G 58-0179, from the 2nd Wing at Barksdale AFB, Louisiana. The art is dedicated to a WWII B-17 "MISS BEA HAVIN"; and as it is signed by Cooke, one might assume that the airplane was assigned to the 93rd Bomb Wing when the art was applied. *Walker*

SMAUG'S REVENGE is B-52H 60-0010, from the 7th Wing at Carswell AFB. The artwork combines a dragon – presumably "Smaug" from J. R. R. Tolkien's The Hobbit – and a B-52. A reference to the tremendous amount of smoke the B-52, even a TF-33-powered "H" model, puts out may have been intended as well. *Mark Lewis*

B-52H 61-0003, a 28th Bomb Wing BUFF, wore these markings when photographed at Offutt AFB in 1979. *Don Logan*

JUNKYARD DOG was B-52H 60-0016 from the 7th Wing at Carswell AFB, Texas. While the regs requiring nose art to be "gender-neutral" prevail, this would seem to apply to the male gender as well as the female. *Mark Lewis*

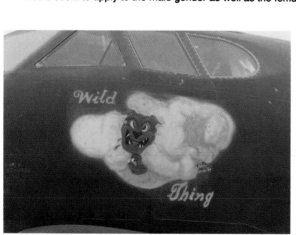

THE ALBATROSS was B-52H 61-0009 with the 92nd Bomb Wing. *92 BW*

WILD THING, is B-52G 57-6486, a 93rd Bomb Wing BUFF. *Walker*

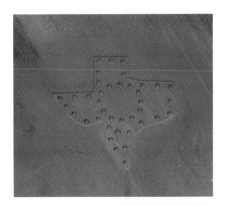

In addition, "The Kelly Crew" repaired holes in 58-0253's skin with patches shaped like the states of Texas and Oklahoma. *Walker*

Major Horace S. Carswell, posthumous Medal of Honor recipient for whom Carswell AFB is named, is remembered on B-52H 60-0007 from the 7th Wing. Balls7 was the last 7th Wing aircraft to leave Carswell, doing so on 18 December 1992 with Lt.Gen. Martin Ryan Jr., 8th AF Commander, at the controls. *Jim Dunn*

B-52G 58-0253, the 42nd BW's APPETITE FOR DESTRUCTION, completed 52 Gulf War sorties from Jeddah and received minor battle damage in the form of small shrapnel holes –mostly in the fuselage and left wing. Repairs were affected in the field by the 2954th CLSS from Kelly AFB, TX, who also had a hand in the amazing variety of graffiti scrawled on the bomber. Walker

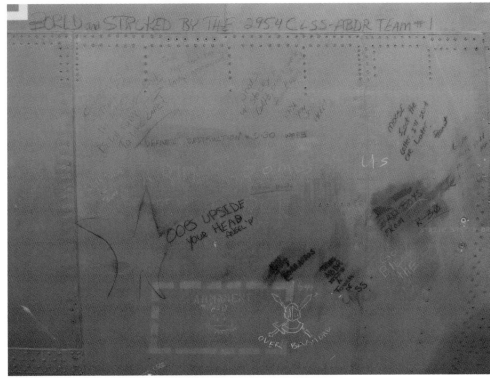

CHAPTER 3
F-111/FB-111 AARDVARK

EF-111A Raven 66-0055, of the 66th ECW, 42nd ECS, was photographed after returning home from desert duty. A 42nd ECS EF-111A is reported to have scored an aeril victory over an Iraqi Mirage F1 on 17 January 1991. While pursuing the unarmed EF-111 at a very low level the Mirage collided with the ground. Paul Bigelow

Here a 366th TFW, 390th ECS EF-111A radar jammer is seen taxiing out for another Desert Storm sortie. The EF-111A is a conversion of the F-111A for the Suppression of Enemy Air Defenses (SEAD) mission. *366 TFW*

FB-111A 67-7195 of the 509th Bomb Wing was named BIG STINK after a 509th Composite Wing B-29, with the art authentically reproduced, albeit on a much smaller scale. *Jim Dunn*

DAVE'S DREAM, the B-29 used in the 1946 Operation Crossroads atomic bomb test, was honored on the other side of FB-111A 67-7195. The art, which is a bit worn, depicts the 509th Group Superfortress on the left and the FB-111A to the right of the mushroom cloud. *Jim Dunn*

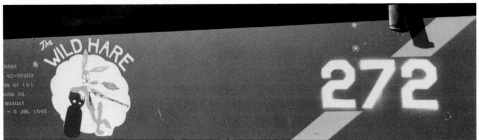

WILD HARE, FB-111A 68-0272, was also owned by the 509th Bomb Wing, which deactivated in 1990. *Wally Van Winkle*

The 509th Bomb Wing's practice of reproducing WWII artwork on their FB-111As was continued two-fold on 67-7196. RUPTURED DUCK was named after a 389th BG B-24H that had in turn adopted the name from one of the Doolittle's Raiders B-25Bs. *Jim Meehan*

THE WILD HARE F-111E 68-0014 from the 20th TFW, 55th TFS at RAF Upper Heyford carries 24 mission symbols. The 20th TFW deployed aircraft to Incerlik, Turkey from August 1990 to March 1991. *Walker*

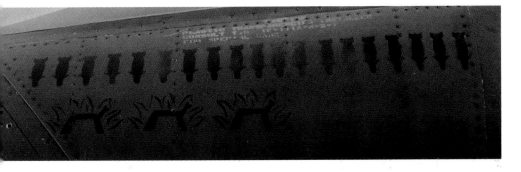

STRAIGHT FLUSH Gulf War mission symbols on F-111F 72-1450, from the 48th TFW based at RAF Lakenheath, consist of 19 bomb silhouettes and 3 symbols representing hardened aircraft shelters being pierced by laser guided bombs. F-111Fs flew over 2500 Gulf War sorties, delivering their ordnance with a very high degree of accuracy. *Paul Bigelow*

FB-111A 69-6503 STRAIGHT FLUSH, 509th BW was named for a 509th Composite Wing B-29, 44-27301 – information that was carried on the nose gear door beside the artwork. *Wally Van Winkle*

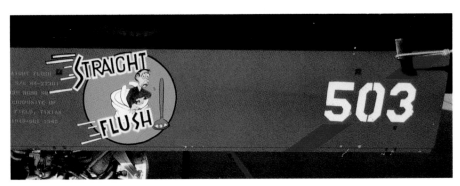

FB-111A 68-0249 LITTLE JOE was the final 380th BW "FB" retired. She was flown to AMARC, Davis-Monthan AFB, on 10 July 1991 by Wing Commander Col. J. Paul Malandrino. "Little Joe" is slang for a dice roll of 4. *Jerry Fugere*

MOONLIGHT MAID, now a bit faded, adorns FB-111A 67-0163, 380th BW. Not one of the FB-111As modified to F-111G standards, 67-0163 was delivered to AMARC on 2 July 1991. *Wally Van Winkle*

SILVER LADY, FB-111A 68-0250 also last served with the 380th BW at Plattsburgh AFB, New York. She was named for a 380th BG B-24, 44-40371. *Wally Van Winkle*

WEE BEE JAMMIN was applied by the 42nd AMU to EF-111A 66-0055, of the 66th Electronic Combat Wing, 42nd Electronic Combat Squadron, home based at Upper Heyford. *Paul Bigelow*

F-111D 68-0127 from the 27th TFW at Cannon AFB, New Mexico, was named CITY OF CLOVIS after the nearby community. The 27th's F-111Ds are being replaced with "new" F-111Gs – modified FB-111As. *Wally Van Winkle*

F-111D 68-0111, 27 TFW, has had portions of the serial number and the "F" in the Air Force "AF" highlighted, and a "D" added to make sure everyone knows what kind of jet it is. *Wally Van Winkle*

Mission symbols on EF-111A 66-0055 are lightning bolts, a popular motif for the jammers. Each bolt apparently represents 5 sorties. *Paul Bigelow*

EF-111A mission symbols, this time in the form of a radar dish with a lightning bolt through it, were applied below the canopy on the pilots side only on 366 TFW, 390 ECS aircraft. Here 67-0033 also carries the small Desert Storm, Rockin' Iraq logo below the windscreen. *366 TFW*

CHAPTER 4
C-135 STRATOTANKER

The first C-135 was delivered in 1957, and it is expected that the KC-135 tanker fleet will fly until at least 2035. The EC-135 Airborne Command Posts are being put into storage, with the thawing of the Cold War, alongside the older KC-135As – the future of the U.S. Air Force's primary tanker lies in re-engined and updated models like the KC-135E, and the KC-135R. Pictured here is KC-135E 57-1484 PHOENIX PHANTACY of the 161st ARG. *Walker*

ON TAP, KC-135A 63-8881, was known as "Jenny On Tap" while with the 380th Bomb Wing. Part of the original artwork has been removed or worn away. Unusual for a tanker, her Desert Storm mission markers are bombs. Camel symbols are depicted with both the Flying Boom and probe and drogue refueling basket, representing both systems the KC-135 can use to transfer fuel. ON TAP wears the badge of the 376th Organizational Maintenance Squadron, a subordinate unit of the 376th Strategic Wing at Kadena. *Brian C. Rogers*

EIGHT BALL, KC-135A 63-8000 was operated by the 22nd Air Refueling Wing in 1988. The 22nd ARW's KC-135 squadron was deactivated on Dec. 1, 1989. *Paul Bigelow*

AMERICAN MAID is a KC-135A, 57-2602, from the 7th Wing at Carswell AFB, Texas. She was captured on film in June 1989, and was re-engined with TF-33 turbofans in August 1991 to become a KC-135E. *Wally Van Winkle*

BOSS HOG, KC-135A 56-3625, is another 96th W tanker. The same name and artwork appear on a 96th BW B-1B. *Don Logan*

KC-135A 56-3601 of the 7th ARS, 7th Wing wore this patriotic artwork in March 1992. *Brian C. Rogers via Joe Bruch*

VALHALLA EXPRESS is KC-135A 63-3538. According to Norse mythology, Valhalla is the great hall where the souls of brave warriors slain in battle are taken by the Valkyrie to feast and swap war stories. *L. N. Paul*

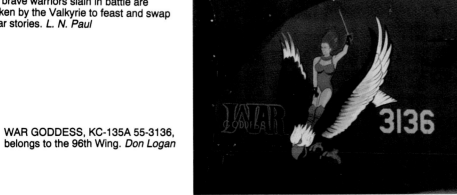

WAR GODDESS, KC-135A 55-3136, belongs to the 96th Wing. *Don Logan*

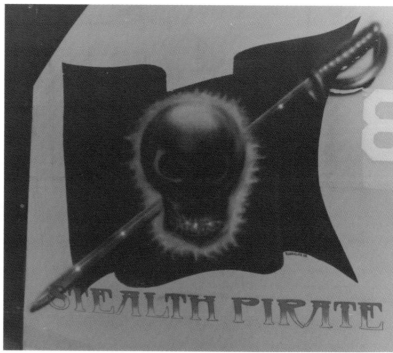

Nose art with an American Indian flavor, KAH WAM DE MEH is KC-135A 56-3644. Writing beneath the artwork, "I GAZE MEAT", might be a literal translation of the name. *Walker*

An impressive jolly roger-like design comprised of a sinister looking black skull and a gleaming cutlass adorns KC-135A 63-8044, STEALTH PIRATE of the 93 Bomb Wing. Of all the fine qualities one could attribute to the C-135 family of aircraft, stealth – and what that word has come to represent in the age of "low observables" technology –would not usually come towards the top of the list. *93 BW/USAF*

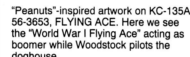

"Peanuts"-inspired artwork on KC-135A 56-3653, FLYING ACE. Here we see the "World War I Flying Ace" acting as boomer while Woodstock pilots the doghouse.

GRIM REAPER, KC-135A 55-3142, 93 BW, carries artwork originally found on a 97th Bomb Group B-17 that served with distinction over North Africa. A version of the same nose art also appeared on a 2nd Wing B-52G (59-2582). *93 BW/USAF*

This attractive piece of airbrush work appeared on KC-135A, 61-0288, named WARRIOR, 93rd Bomb Wing. 93rd BW/ USAF

KC-135A 58-0033 KNIGHT RIDER received this artwork while with the 7th Wing. *Walker*

ARKANSAS EAGLE is KC-135A 62-3498 from the 97th Bomb Wing at Eaker AFB. *Walker*

KC-135A 64-14838 THUNDERBIRD, of the 93rd Bomb Wing, is one of the newest KC-135's – delivered to the U.S. Air Force in 1964. *93 BW/ USAF*

YANKEE CLIPPER is a 96th Wing KC-135A, 56-3635. *Don Logan*

This elaborate nose art adorns KC-135A 60-0326 MIDNIGHT EXPRESS from the 379th Bomb Wing, at Wurtsmith AFB, Michigan. *Walker*

An armadillo with an attitude, TEXAS ARM-A-DILLO is 96th W KC-135A, 62-3532. *Don Logan*

RISKY BUSINESS is a good way to describe the art of aerial refueling, but this difficult task is accomplished day or night, in all kinds of weather every day by the highly skilled and well trained tanker crews. KC-135A 63-8019 belongs to the 96th Wing at Dyess. *Don Logan*

KC-135A 57-2591 ONE TIME GOOD DEAL belonged to the 410th Bomb Wing in 1991. *Brian C. Rogers*

KC-135A 62-3539, RUNNING FREE, 96th Bomb Wing. *Don Logan*

FLEX-A-BULL is KC-135A 58-0114 from the 96th Wing. *Don Logan*

KC-135A 57-1475 of the 161 ARG (now "Phoenix Cardinals", a re-engined E-model with the same unit), was named GOOD TO THE LAST DROP in 1989. The art shows coffee being poured into the air refueling receiver on a B-52. *Wally Van Winkle*

BIG BAD BOOM is another 410th BW KC-135A, 56-3637. *Bob Shane*

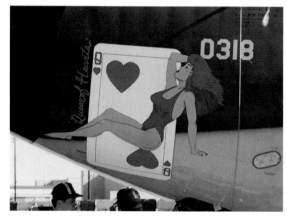

KC-135A 60-0318, QUEEN OF HEARTS, is operated by the 96th Wing at Dyess AFB. The nose art has been changed, but the name remains the same. *Don Logan*

Another version of the QUEEN OF HEARTS artwork was carried on KC-135A 60-0318, still with the 96th Wing. *Don Logan*

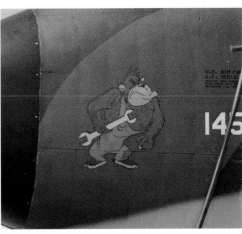

STEAMIN' N' SCREAMIN' was one of the 96th Wing's KC-135As, 55-3137. The name alludes to the J57-powered tanker's use of water injection to boost thrust briefly for takeoff; a noisy, smoky and somewhat perilous practice that will slowly fade into history as the "Steam Jets" are retired or reengined. *Don Logan*

OL' LIGHTNEN is a KC-135E, 58-0005, from the 190th ARG. The name was derived from an incident where the tanker was struck by lightning during a thunderstorm at Forbes Field in Topeka, Kansas. *Brian C. Rogers*

KC-135E 57-1458 carried this artwork in the gulf. *Brian C. Rogers*

Artwork on KC-135E 57-1475 PHOENIX CARDINALS of the 161st ARG shows support for the local pro football team. *Bob Shane*

KC-135E 57-1512, KUKAI MARU came from the 452nd Air Refueling Wing (AFRES) at March AFB. She is reputed to be "The Haunted Tanker." Strange noises and unexplained footsteps might be heard by guards when this aircraft is on alert; in a hangar where it is parked lights would turn on or off by themselves. *Brian C. Rogers*

The nose art on KC-135E 56-3650 NUMBAH I tells a lot about the experiences of the aircraft and her crew. "Fluffed and Buffed" refers to the crew chief, who keeps his hair in immaculate condition. A bird being ingested recalls when the number 2 engine got FODed out near Wake Island. The Pease International Tradeport sign reflects recent activities at the 157th ARG's home since the closing of Pease AFB. St Jean's is a watering hole near Bitburg, a favorite TDY, but the purpose of the banana is unclear. Soon the New Hampshire ANG will receive KC-135Rs and their E models will go to a unit in California. *Walker*

KI-O' TE-ES GAS-E-ES, is KC-135E 56-3641 from the 190th Air Refueling Group, The Kansas Coyotes. *Brian C. Rogers*

ARCTIC TRAVELLER is a KC-135E, 57-1448, from the 168th Air Refueling Group at Eielson AFB, Alaska. *David F. Brown*

The nose art on JERSEY GIRL, KC-135E 58-0087, 170th ARG, has gone through a series of modifications. The original artwork, much like the current version, featured an eye-catching bikini-clad female. During the early days of Desert Shield, she was painted over with a full length black dress, white belt and pearl necklace to avoid offending the locals in the Gulf region. After the war, crew chief TSgt Samuel Fleming contacted the original artist, Gary Campbell, who created an entirely new painting returning Jersey Girl to her former glory. *170 ARG/New Jersey ANG*

KC-135E 56-3631 LEAP-N-LIZARD displays camel mission symbols from the Gulf War, and the slogan "Saddam cries when the lizard flies. Humping to please." *Brian C. Rogers*

While participating in Operation Desert Storm, KC-135E 58-0013 became caught in the wake turbulence of another tanker and was so violently shaken that both engines were torn from the left wing. The plane was safely recovered, due to the skill of the crew and the inherent strength of the airframe, and was repaired by the 2953rd Combat & Logistics Support Squadron – who applied these markings for the FLIGHT OF THE PHOENIX back to the States. The dead cat eulogized here expired on board 0013 while the aircraft was awaiting repair in Saudi Arabia. *Steve Link*

KC-135E 57-2595 KEYSTONE LADY is based at Greater Pittsburgh International Airport with the 171 Air Refueling Wing, Pennsylvania Air National Guard. Adad numerals representing the tanker's serial number were applied for service in the Gulf. *David F. Brown*

KC-135E 57-1495 BLACK BIRD-WE DELIVER is a 161st Air Refueling Group tanker based at Sky Harbor International Airport in Phoenix. *Walker*

WORK'N GIRL is a KC-135E, 58-0006, from the 151st ARG, 191st ARS, Utah Air National Guard. *Brian C. Rogers via Bruch*

LEAPING LIZARD, with art depicting some kind of dragon taking to the skies, is KC-135E 57-1510 from the 191st Air Refueling Squadron. *Paul Bigelow*

From the 134th ARG, Tennessee ANG, KC-135E 57-1455 IRON MAIDEN carries popular artwork derived from advertisements for RumpleMinze Peppermint Schnapps. Stencilled birds reportedly represent missions out of Dubai, in the United Arab Emirates, with the 1713th Air Refueling Wing (Provisional). *Brian C. Rogers*

KC-135E 55-3146 THE CITY OF COLUMBUS belonged to the 160th Air Refueling Wing, Ohio ANG, in 1988. *Wally Van Winkle*

A rodeo rider on a fearsome red-eyed horse adorns WILD THANG, KC-135E, 57-1496 from the 161 ARG, Arizona ANG. *Rene Francillon*

Historic KC-135R 62-3554 CHEROKEE ROSE set 16 time-to-climb records on 19 October 1988 at Robins AFB, Georgia, flown by crews from McConnell, Grand Forks, Altus and Robins. The art was painted prior to the record attempts, and was painstakingly masked over when the tanker was repainted into the camo gray scheme. As of March 1992 she was still with the 19th ARW. *Brian C. Rogers via Bruch*

KC-135E 56-3643 HIGH OCTANE TAZ belongs to the 134th Air Refueling Group, Tennessee ANG. A total of ten camel symbols comprise this aircraft's Gulf War mission tally. MISS HIGH OCTANE TAZ, a Tasmanian She-devil, is carried on the starboard side of 3643. *Steve Link*

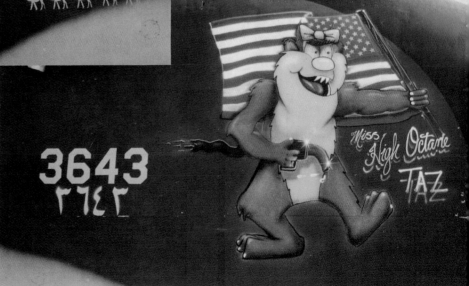

KC-135R 61-0264 EASY RIDER is another 19th ARW aircraft. *Brian C. Rogers via Bruch*

BOEING LADY is a 19th ARW KC-135R, 63-7977. Two squadrons of KC-135Rs-the 99th and 912th-are operated by the 19th Air Refueling Wing. *Brian C. Rogers via Bruch*

One of two KC-135Rs at Grand Forks sharing the same name was ESPRIT DE CORPS 59-1453. The tail number may have been added to distinguish this tanker from 61-0275, though their artwork was quite different. All of the 319th Wing's nose art was removed in 1992. Wally Van Winkle

This artwork is found inside KC-135E 55-3143 on the bulkhead just forward of the cargo door. The branding iron is shaped like the state of Arizona with a star over Phoenix where the 161st ARG is based. Walker

KC-135E 58-0115, from the 170th ARG, New Jersey ANG, is named SHANTY IRISH. Crew chief TSgt Patrick McDermott defines Shanty Irish as "a hard working, hard partying, fun loving bunch of people." The artwork, featuring a shamrock and a leprechaun, was applied by SSgt John Hutton – a former crew member on 0115. *170 ARG/New Jersey ANG*

A reluctant Wile E. Coyote, flying under the power of an "Acme" F-108 engine, is the subject of the artwork on KC-135R 62-3569, Sky Runner from the 19th ARW. *Brian C. Rogers via Bruch*

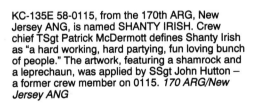

GLADIATOR is KC-135R 57-2597 of the 19th ARW. The unit's winged sword insignia is carried on the Gladiator's shield. *Brian C. Rogers via Bruch*

Named in honor of the local pro basketball team, PHOENIX SUNS is 161 ARG KC-135E 61-0281, based at Sky Harbor. Suns star Lonnie Hawkins "autographed" the aircraft just inside the crew door. Walker

KC-135E 56-3638 HAWG WILD is another example from the 161st ARG. Rene Francillon

Mission symbols on KC-135E 56-3638. Camels with reindeer antlers represent Desert Shield missions flown during Christmas week. Rene Francillon

Censorship in action. KC-135R 61-0275 ESPRIT DE CORPS from the 319th Wing's 905th Air Refueling Squadron had her nose art depicting a female clad in a partially unzipped bomber jacket – covered up during a 1991 visit to Beale AFB. Jim Dunn

EAGLE DANCER is KC-135E 57-1452, from the 161st ARG, Arizona ANG. The artwork, (drawing inspiration from the American Indian culture that abounds in the Southwest), is signed by artist Louis Santellan and dated 14 Feb '92. Walker

COBRA JET was KC-135Q 58-0103 from the 9th SRW. Mission symbols included Maltese Crosses – also utilized in the 9th SRW's tail markings, tracing the unit's heritage back to the lst Aero Squadron of World War I – as well as the more widely used camels. Brian C. Rogers

Another variation on the use of camels as mission symbols, found on KC-135E 57-1484 PHOENIX PHANTACY. A large, winged camel equipped with a refueling boom and 12 smaller red camels with open mouths represent 12 sorties during Operation Desert Shield. Walker

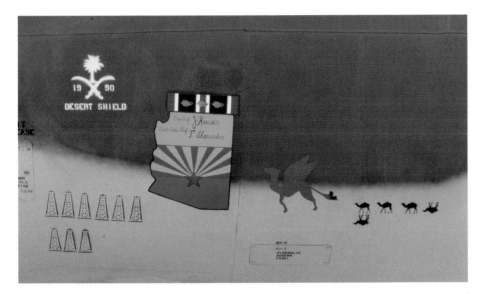

Early in Operation Desert Shield the crew of this 161st ARG KC-135E, 57-1433, used oil derricks as mission markings. The upside down camels represent air aborts. Walker

Lightning bolts serve as mission symbols on 161st ARG KC-135E 57-1484, reputed to be "the first tanker in Desert Shield." The airplane was in Germany when Iraqi troops invaded Kuwait, and took part in the first movements of U.S. personnel and equipment into the region. Walker

KC-135Q 58-0074 JEZEBEL is another 9th Wing tanker. Jim Dunn

LIL MO GAS, KC-135Q 58-0129, works for "Flying Q Gasoline" with the 9th Wing out of Beale AFB. Jim Dunn

KC-135Q 58-0125 IRON MAIDEN also belongs to the 9th Wing. Jim Dunn

BAD COMPANY is KC-135Q 59-1513, 9th Wing. Walker

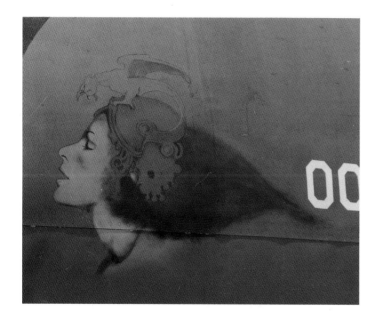

This art is found on KC-135Q 58-0071, from the 9th Wing. Jim Dunn

KC-135Q 59-1520, from the 9th Wing, carries this rendition of the mythological winged horse Pegasus. N. Donald

CITY OF GRASS VALLEY is 9th SRW KC-135Q 58-0084, named for a community northeast of Beale AFB. Artwork applied during Desert Storm shows a well-known cartoon mouse with a message for Iraq. Brian C. Rogers

CITY OF WHEATLAND is a 9th Wing (previously the 9th Strategic Reconnaissance Wing) KC-135Q 58-0088, named for a community southwest of Beale AFB. Jim Meehan

KC-135R 63-8008 FLYING DUTCHMAN flys the banner of the 19th Air Refueling Wing, based at Robins AFB, Georgia. Walker

Another example of 9th SRW Desert Storm markings, this time on KC-135Q 59-1470. Jim Dunn

THE OLD GRAY HARE is a KC-135R, 57-1439, from the 92nd Wing at Fairchild AFB. The artwork, featuring Bugs Bunny and the aircraft rendered in 1930's cartoon syle, is dedicated to the memory of Sgt. Hector Jimenez, Jr. – a tanker crew chief who lost his life while deployed to Moron, Spain during Operation Desert Storm. Steve Link

MISS SPOKANE, KC-135R 62-3578, is seen here on 22 May 1992, carrying the new AMC badge and the 92nd Bomb Wing's "Seattle Seahawk" logo along with a nice piece of nose art which originally appeared on a 92nd BG B-29 (44-27332) in Korea. Jim Meehan

Nose art on KC-135Q 58-0125, from the 9th SRW, was a rather demented-looking Bart Simpson with sharp pointed teeth. Jim Meehan

HOOVER is KC-135R 59-1517 from the 28th Wing. The "R"-model's big F-108-CF-l00 engines will suck up just about anything within their reach, as illustrated by this whimsical creature. Jim Meehan

KC-135R 59-1478 was named COMMAND DECISION while serving with the 380th Bomb Wing in 1989. L.N. Paul

Attractive nose art on KC-135R 58-0076 SPIRIT OF 76 from the 92nd Bomb Wing at Fairchild AFB, moments before being stripped during PDM. Steve Link

The original COMMAND DECISION was this 19th Bomb Group B-29, 44-87657. She flew over 120 missions and downed five MiGs during the Korean War. Though not on a par with "Memphis Belle", this artwork has been reproduced on many different aircraft. AFM

KC-135R 62-3514 NIGHT RIDER II, from the 305th ARW, carries this simple but effective "shady lady" artwork. Steve Link

These markings are found on KC-135R 62-3514 near the crew entry door. The exact significance of the moose and scorpion symbols is not clear. Steve Link

Mission symbols on the shadow side of KC-135E 59-1516 SWEET SIXTEEN, 190th ARG Kansas ANG; black "compact" camels for Desert Shield, red for Desert Storm – a grand total of 63 refueling sorties. Walker

WESTERN CHALLENGE is a KC-135R, 63-7977, belonging to the 19th Air Refueling Wing. Jim Meehan

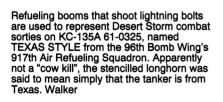

A depiction of the feminine gender that few would find offensive, MISTRESS OF THE SKY was KC-135R, 62-3577, 93rd Bomb Wing. At this time the 93rd operated a mixed fleet of KC-135As and KC-135Rs, as well as B-52Gs. 93rd BW/USAF

KC-135R 58-0051 KE ALI'I, HAWAII PARADISE OF THE PACIFIC was operated by the 93rd Bomb Wing in 1991. In Hawaiian, "Ke ali i" can be used to say that something is the best of it's kind, or in referring to royalty. Jim Dunn

Refueling booms that shoot lightning bolts are used to represent Desert Storm combat sorties on KC-135A 61-0325, named TEXAS STYLE from the 96th Bomb Wing's 917th Air Refueling Squadron. Apparently not a "cow kill", the stencilled longhorn was said to mean simply that the tanker is from Texas. Walker

Unusual markings on 42nd BW KC-135R 57-1469, named "Centurion" – what appears to be a squirrel climbing the Eiffel Tower, with the words "Desert Storm French Connection." More commonly applied Desert Shield logo and camel mission tally are also carried. Dan Tasca

C-135E 60-0372, named BIG BYRD for obvious reasons by her crew chief, is utilized by the 4950th Test Wing at Wright Patterson AFB – apparently working with the Milstar satellite program. This aircraft served as an EC-135N ARIA platform for a time, but has since had the ARIA equipment and the extra large radome removed. Walker

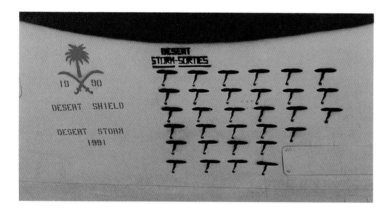

Another variation on Desert Storm tanker mission symbols, these markings appeared on KC-135A 60-0350, named YOUNG RIDER while serving with the 5th Bomb Wing. This aircraft is now a KC-135R, having been re-engined in October 1991. Mike Hill

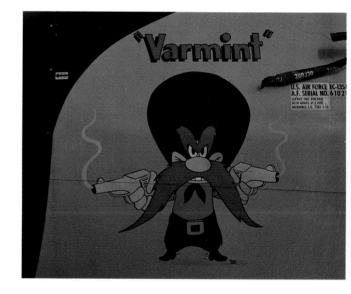

EC-135L 61-0283 VARMINT was operated by the 305th Air Refueling Wing out of Grissom AFB, Indiana. Modified from basic KC-135As, EC-135Ls were configured to provide an airborne relay platform for coded communication used for the launch and control of Minuteman ICBMs. Walker

When U.S. forces began returning home from the Gulf War this yellow ribbon was painted below the boomer's compartment on 157th ARG KC-135E 57-1505, where it would greet any aircraft taking on fuel. KC-135's from the 170th ARG and 191st ARS carried similar markings. Walker

VARMINT carries these mission symbols, in the form of Scud missile Transporter-Erector-Launchers, earned during the war in the Gulf. Deployed to King Khalid International Airport in Riyadh, the EC-135L was well suited to perform as a relay between satellites and ground stations to accellerate the transmission of Scud launch information. Walker

ROLLIN THUNDER is EC-135A 61-0262, from the 28th Wing at Ellsworth AFB, South Dakota. This Airborne Command Post was retired in January 1992 to be placed on static display at Ellsworth. Jim Meehan

NIGHT ANGEL was EC-135H 61-0286 from the l0th Airborne Command and Control Squadron. This aircraft now serves as a GEC-135H permanently grounded training airframe at the Sheppard Technical Training Center in Wichita Falls, TX. Paul Bigelow

WC-135B 61-2665 was named STARCASTER. At that time she belonged to the 55th Weather Reconnaissance Squadron at McClellan AFB. *Steve Link*

EC-135H 61-0291 was named THE ANGLIAN LION while serving with the l0th ACCS at RAF Mildenhall. Retired from service in 1991, she was flown to the Aerospace Maintenance And Regeneration Center at Davis Monthan AFB and methodically cut apart to study the effects of corrosion and fatigue on the skin and structure of the aircraft. Knowledge gained will help maintain the C-135 fleet well into the 21st century. Wally Van Winkle

KC-135A 55-3130, OLE GRANDAD, of the 7th ARS at Carswell AFB, was the oldest operational tanker prior to being retired in December of 1992 - accepted on 2 August 1957. The handful of more elderly C-135 airframes serve as EC-135s or NKC-135 test ships. OLE GRANDAD is now a display item at March AFB, California. *Walker*

CHAPTER 5
KC-10A EXTENDER

KC-10A 84-0189 ACE OF SPADES from the 22nd ARW was a frequent visitor to Diego Garcia during Operations Desert Shield/Desert Storm. KC-10's performed the dual-role of air refueling tanker and airlifter, maintaining a 95% mission capable rate throughout the conflict. Jim Dunn

ACE OF SPADES is seen off-loading cargo on the island of Diego Garcia in the Indian Ocean. 42 BW via Dan Tasca

LOUISIANA YARD DOG, KC-10A 85-0034 belongs to the 2nd Wing. As illustrated, a "Louisiana Yard Dog" is a 'gator with an attitude. Jim Meehan

LONE WOLF appeared on KC-10A 86-0037, 4th Wing. Wally Van Winkle

SPIRIT OF 76, 22nd Air Refueling Wing KC-10A 83-0076 is adorned with this patriotic nose art. Jim Dunn

Another KC-10A from the 68th ARW, LUCKY LISA is 86-0030. David F. Brown

Some KC-10As still wear the blue and white over gray paint scheme they were delivered in, such as 83-0075 INTERNATIONAL EXPRESS from the 2nd Wing at Barksdale AFB. Walker

The artwork on WABBIT TWANSIT, KC-10A 79-1974, depicts Bugs Bunny and Porky Pig blasting off aboard a happy KC-10. Inspiration for this 22nd ARW nose art came from a WW II B-24 of the same name, that bore a similar painting with the Warner Brothers cartoon stars riding a rocket. Jim Dunn

PEACE MAKER, KC-10A 86-0056, from the 68th ARW at Seymour Johnson AFB, carries 67 mission marks from Desert Storm. Forty-three KC-10As were deployed to the theater of operations, with the rest of the 57-ship fleet involved in long range resupply missions from the U. S. to the Gulf. David F. Brown

CHAPTER 6
A-10 WARTHOG

With Col. Bob Efferson, commander of the 926 TFG, at the controls 77-0255 took a 57mm anti-aircraft hit on 5 February 1991 while hunting Scuds near the Jordanian border in western Iraq. With no less than 378 holes in the aircraft, leaking fuel and hydraulic fluid, with damaged flight controls and one engine faltering, Col. Efferson skillfully recovered the damaged 'Hog at the forward operating location (FOL) at Al Jouf. A battle damage repair team from the Sacramento ALC made extensive repairs to CAMEL JOCKEY and the jet was returned to service in time to fly additional combat missions. Now retired, 77-0255 will be placed on static display at NAS New Orleans. Tammy Lulei, 926th FG

Kevin Smith painted CAMEL JOCKEY on A-10A 77-0255, 926 TFG, for crew chief SSgt Jack Atkins. The aircraft is assigned to Lt. Col Tom Coleman. Kill markings attest to the demise of 8 tanks, 2 armored vehicles, 10 artillery pieces, 2 Scud launchers, 6 radar sites and 8 trucks. Tammy Lulei, 926th FG

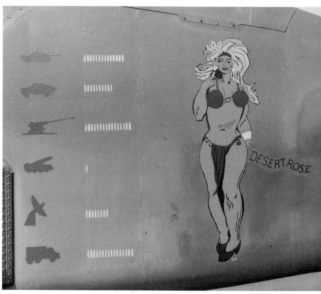

DESERT ROSE is A-10A 77-0273 of the 926 TFG. The crew Chief is SSgt Eric Rester; pilot, Maj. Jim Rose. The initials "G.C." near the blonde's foot indicate that she was painted by TSgt George Cunnikin. Kills consist of 14 tanks, 10 armored vehicles, 16 artillery pieces, one Scud launcher, 8 radar sites and 16 trucks. Tammy Lulei, 926th FG

This OPERATION DESERT STORM patch, also painted by George Cunnikin appears on A-10A 77-0272, 926 TFG, crewed by MSgt Farrel Avist and flown by Maj. Richard Sachitano. Kills include 9 tanks, 5 armored vehicles, 8 artillery pieces, one Scud launcher, 4 radar sites and 10 trucks. Tammy Lulei, 926th FG

The left side of A-10A 77-0272 carries the crawfish found on several of the New Orleans aircraft, but this DESERT DOC version is armed with a stethoscope as well as a "voo doo" lightning bolt. The names of pilot, and Flight Surgeon, Richard Sachitano's wife and children are also carried. Tammy Lulei, 926 FG

BELLE OF NEW ORLEANS incorporates a tip of the proverbial hat to the 926 TFG's home at NAS New Orleans and an almost nude female reclining on a crescent moon. A-10A 77-0269 carried this nose art into battle, the kill tally indicating 7 tanks, 4 armored vehicles, 7 artillery pieces, 4 Scud launchers, 3 radar sites and 8 trucks destroyed. Tammy Lulei, 926th FG

A large American flag and the names of pilot Maj. George "Sonny" Rasar's family grace the starboard side of 77-0240, along with kill markings representing 10 tanks, 5 armored vehicles, 9 artillery pieces, one Scud launcher, 4 radar sites and 11 trucks. Bob Shane

IRAQI NIGHTMARE is A-10A 77-0266, 926 TFG. The artwork – applied by SSgt Charles Lohr and Sgt Denise Mazzola –depicts a rather gruesome looking soldier who's face seems to be melting away, peering through a hole in the side of the aircraft. IRAQI NIGHTMARE lived up to the name, dispatching 22 tanks, 14 armored vehicles, 24 artillery pieces, one Scud launcher, 8 radar sites and 24 trucks. Tammy Lulei, 926 FG

A-10A 77-0260 LADY LUCK, MRS. ROBIN is named for the wife of crew chief TSgt Maurice Arabie, with the names of his children carried on three petals of a white shamrock. Assigned to pilot Capt. Ed Kinney, this 926 TFG A-10 accounted for 14 tanks, 8 armored vehicles, 16 artillery pieces, 2 Scud launchers, 4 radar sites and 14 trucks. Tammy Lulei, 926 FG

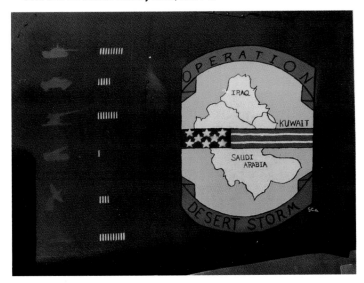

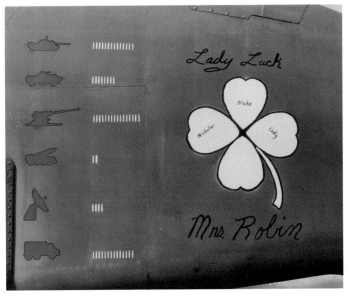

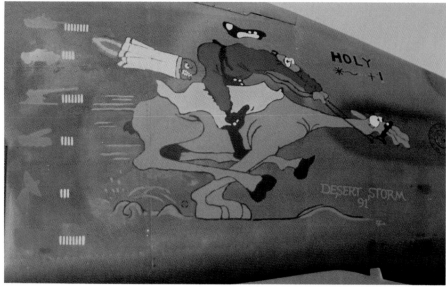

A-10A 77-0271, HOLY *#&+!, belonging to the 926th TFG, was assigned to Maj. Randy Falcon. Crew chief George Cunnikin applied the artwork. Kill markings claim 8 tanks, 4 vehicles, 7 artillery pieces, 4 Scud launchers, 3 radar sites and 8 trucks destroyed. David F. Brown

The right side of CHOPPER POPPER, 77-0205, bears the flags of all the coalition nations; plus kill markings for 24 trucks, 11 radar sites, 10 Scud launchers, 15 artillery pieces, 14 vehicles, 27 tanks and one helicopter. Warthogs scored the only two air-to-air gun kills of the war. Tammy Lulei, 926 FG

A-10A 77-0240 LUCKY SUN DOG wears the 926th TFG's Desert Storm crawfish, this time clutching a tank, as well as a partial pin-up inside the ladder door. Tammy Lulei, 926 FG

Captain Bob Swain shot down an Iraqi B0-105 observation helicopter on 6 February, 1991, using the A-10's GAU-8A 30mm cannon. A-10A 77-0205 CHOPPER POPPER, 926 TFG, carries the kill flag and obligatory crawfish holding a helicopter in one claw, though some reports list another 926 TFG aircraft – 77-0275 – as the Warthog that downed the helicopter. 77-0205 is slated to be put on static display at the Armament Museum, Eglin AFB, Florida. Tammy Lulei, 926 FG

The starboard side of A-10A 79-0096 bore this nose art and the name WICKED SENSATION. On a 353rd TFS Panthers aircraft it seems logical that the grim reaper would be accompanied by a panther. 354 TFW/USAF

Captain Jim Callaway painted this Warthog's head on his A-10A, 77-0275, 926 TFG. Kill markings denote 16 tanks, 8 armored vehicles, 14 artillery pieces, one Scud launcher, 6 radar sites and 17 trucks destroyed. Tammy Lulei, 926 FG

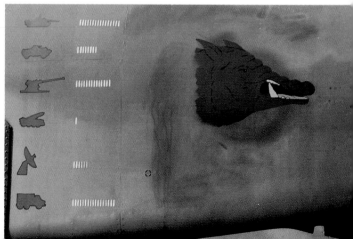

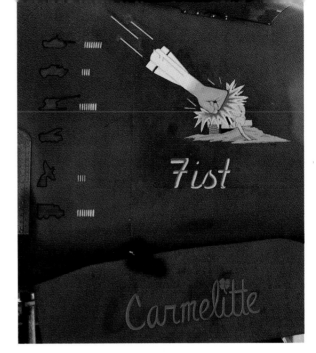

DESERT STORM HEROES is a A-10A 76-0544, 926 TFG, AFRES. This Warthog was assigned to pilot Lt. Col. Lee Brundage, and her crew chief was TSgt Billy Bryant. Kill markings indicate that -544 accounted for 9 tanks, 5 vehicles, 8 artillery pieces, 4 radar sites and 10 trucks. Tammy Lulei, 926 FG

A-10A 76-0540, FIST, from the 926 TFG at NAS New Orleans, carries this artwork depicting a combination Maverick missile and fist smashing a tank. Piloted by Maj. Jim Venturella and crewed by SSgt Jim Marcello, FIST destroyed 8 tanks, 4 armored vehicles, 8 artillery pieces, 4 radar sites and 8 trucks. The aircraft was retired shortly after the Gulf War and is now preserved in the McClellan AFB Museum. Tammy Lulei, 926 FG

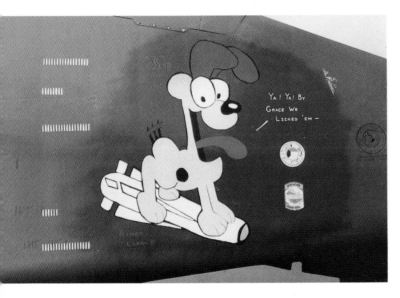

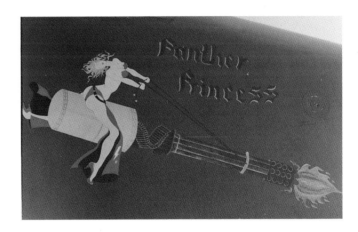

Garfield's pal Odie was painted on A-10A 77-0227, 926 TFG, by the crew chief TSgt Larry Hammer and Kevin Smith. Normally flown by Capt. David Duncan, 77-0227 carries kill markings for 17 tanks, 8 armored vehicles, 18 artillery pieces, 6 radar sites and 18 trucks. Other kills, including one Scud launcher, appear to have been scratched or drawn on the airplane near the red silhouettes. Tammy Lulei, 926 FG

NEW ORLEANS LADY on A-10A 77-0274, 926 TFG. Pilot: Maj. Richard Pauly, crew chief: Bob Farno. The art was applied by MSgt Perry Bonck. This Warthog carries kill markings for 7 tanks, 4 armored vehicles, 7 artillery pieces, 3 radar sites and 8 trucks. Tammy Lulei, 926th FG

Not surprisingly the A-10's massive GAU-8A Avenger 30mm cannon became the focal point of many examples of Gulf War "Hog art." PANTHER PRINCESS, A-10A 78-0594 from the 353rd TFS "Panthers", 354 TFW, features a scantily clad female riding the gun. Of note is the lightning bolt and Roman numeral 2, that could be representative of the Warthog's official and widely disused name – Thunderbolt II. Another high scoring Myrtle Beach aircraft, PANTHER PRINCESS completed 83 combat sorties, killing 3 radar sites, 2 Scud launchers, 9 artillery pieces, 17 tanks, 8 armored vehicles and 28 trucks. 354TFW/USAF

DAWG HAWG, A-10A 79-0097, 354 TFW, 355 TFS, completed 63 sorties and took out 2 radar sites, 5 artillery pieces, 9 tanks, 17 armored vehicles and 16 trucks. 354 TFW/USAF

The nose art applied to A-10A 78-0714 in the Gulf depicts a tank killing LOUISVILLE SLUGGER!. This 354 TFW, 355 TFS machine is credited with 60 combat sorties and the destruction of 4 radar sites, 2 artillery pieces, 3 tanks, 11 armored vehicles and 11 trucks. 354 TFW/USAF

CRESCENT CITY'S DESERT DARLYN is A-10A 77-0268, 926 TFG. Crew chief: TSgt Billy Rester, pilot: Lt. Col. Greg Wilson. Kills include 5 tanks, 3 armored vehicles, 5 artillery pieces, 2 radar sites and 6 trucks David F. Brown

MUD, BLOOD AND NO BEER, the lament of many U.S. and allied personnel stationed in "dry" Arab nations, inspired this artwork on A-10A 79-0115, 354 TFW, 355 TFS, a 66 mission combat veteran that carried kill markings for 2 radar sites, 3 artillery pieces, 13 tanks, 3 armored vehicles and 16 trucks. 354 TFW/USAF

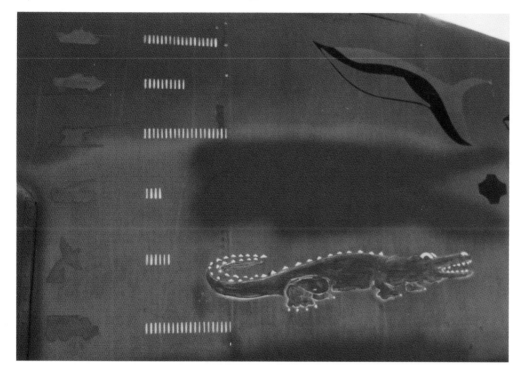

A-10A 78-0582, loaned to the 926th TFG by the 46th TFTS, 917 TFW at Barksdale AFB, wears a 'gator for nose art and an impressive brace of kill markings including 4 Scud launchers. Operating from the FOL at Al Jouf (much closer to the target areas than was the A-10 primary base at King Fahd), the 926th was credited with more kills per aircraft than any other A-10 unit. Jim Dunn

The nose art that flourished during World War II often heaped abuse upon the likes of Adolph Hitler and Hideki Tojo, and several examples of Gulf War art carried on the tradition – this time targeting Saddam Hussein. One such example is HERE COMES THE JUDGE, found on A-10A 79-0112; a 354 TFW, 355 TFS jet that was credited with 61 combat sorties. Kills consisted of 10 artillery pieces, 11 tanks, 3 armored vehicles and 4 trucks. 354 TFW/USAF

Photographed shortly after returning home in April 1991, A-10A 79-0096 carried the name HONEY BUNS on the port side of the fuselage along with kill marking silhouettes representing the destruction of 2 radar sites, no less than 9 Scud launchers, one anti-aircraft gun, 13 tanks, 3 armored vehicles, and 16 trucks. The mission tally – 61 combat sorties – is applied to the inside of the nosewheel door. David F. Brown

MIDNIGHT EXPRESS, A-10A 78-0678, from the 354 TFW, 355 TFS, completed an impressive total of 78 missions while destroying 5 artillery pieces, 11 tanks, 2 armored vehicles and 9 trucks. The artwork draws inspiration from nose art carried on WW II ace John C. Meyer's "Petie" P-51 Mustangs. 354 TFW/USAF

FALCON 1 is A-10A 79-0158 from the 355th TFS "Falcon" squadron of the 354th TFW based at Myrtle Beach AFB, South Carolina. FALCON 1 is credited with 62 missions and the destruction of one radar site, 10 artillery pieces, 14 tanks, 3 armored vehicles and 8 trucks – though at the pilot's request no kills are marked on the aircraft. 354 TFW/USAF

A-10A 78-0622 FEAR NO EVIL deployed to King Fahd Airport at the beginning of Operation Desert Shield with the 354 TFW, 355 TFS in August of 1991. Once the shooting started, 622 flew 71 missions, accounting for one radar site, 7 artillery pieces, 13 tanks, 7 armored vehicles and 3 trucks destroyed. 354 TFW/USAF

The original SECRUT WEAPIN was B-24J 42-100224. AFM

KELLY MARIE'S SECRIT WEAPIN, artwork on A-10A 78-0591, was derived from WW II B-24 nose art. With a total of 55 combat missions this 354 TFW/355 TFS Warthog claimed one radar site, 5 artillery pieces, 12 tanks, 6 armored vehicles and 5 trucks. 354 TFW/USAF

DARIN' DAWNIE is another 354 TFW, 355 TFS A-10A, 78-0710. She completed 61 combat sorties and scored kills against one radar site, 13 artillery pieces, 7 tanks and 8 armored vehicles. 354 TFW/USAF

SHARPER THAN ANY TWO-EDGED SWORD, Biblically inspired nose art on A-10A 79-0163 of the 354th TFW, 355 TFS. This Warthog completed 60 combat missions and destroyed one radar site, 9 artillery pieces, 4 tanks, 4 armored vehicles and 5 trucks. 354 TFW/USAF

LESLIE, THE SEMINOLE WARRIOR, A-10A 78-0724 of the 354 TFW, 355 TFS; with a total of 48 combat sorties, claimed 12 artillery pieces, 2 tanks, 4 armored vehicles and 9 trucks. 354 TFW/USAF

A cartoon BIRD OF PREY prepares to release a bomb in the art carried by A-10A 78-0599. Another 354 TFW, 355 TFS Warthog, BIRD OF PREY flew 65 missions – claiming one radar site, 5 artillery pieces, 9 tanks, 14 armored vehicles and 8 trucks in the process. 354 TFW/USAF

A-10A 78-0662 of the 354 TFW, 355 TFS was named EAT THIS SADDAM! The artwork depicts Sylvester, himself dining on a Tweety Bird, preparing to toss a AGM-65 Maverick. About 5,500 Maverick missiles were expended during the Gulf War. While undertaking 71 combat sorties EAT THIS SADDAM! "plinked" one Scud launcher, 5 tanks, 4 artillery pieces, 3 armored vehicles and 4 trucks. 354 TFW/USAF

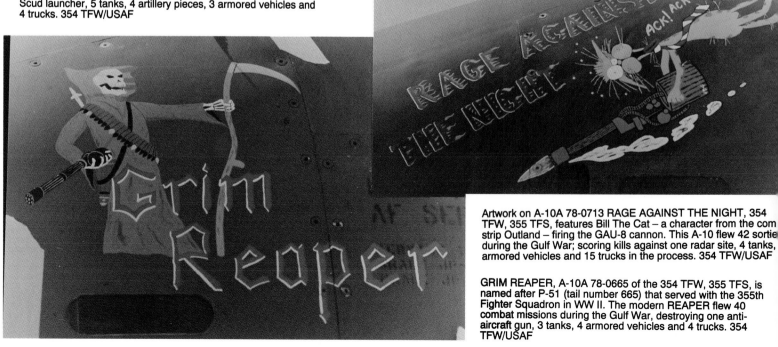

Artwork on A-10A 78-0713 RAGE AGAINST THE NIGHT, 354 TFW, 355 TFS, features Bill The Cat – a character from the comic strip Outland – firing the GAU-8 cannon. This A-10 flew 42 sorties during the Gulf War; scoring kills against one radar site, 4 tanks, armored vehicles and 15 trucks in the process. 354 TFW/USAF

GRIM REAPER, A-10A 78-0665 of the 354 TFW, 355 TFS, is named after P-51 (tail number 665) that served with the 355th Fighter Squadron in WW II. The modern REAPER flew 40 combat missions during the Gulf War, destroying one anti-aircraft gun, 3 tanks, 4 armored vehicles and 4 trucks. 354 TFW/USAF

Captain J. Dobbins, of the 354 TFW, 355 TFS, named his A-10A (79-0160) DOBBER'S STING!. The DOBBER bagged 2 Scud launchers, 11 artillery pieces, 5 tanks, 6 armored vehicles and 4 trucks while completing a total of 76 combat sorties. 354 TFW/ USAF

THE FULL ARMOR OF GOD, A-10A 79-0173 of the 354 TFW, 355 TFS, flew 57 combat missions and reduced the inventory of the Iraqi army by one radar site, 11 artillery pieces, 7 tanks, 5 armored vehicles and 9 trucks. 354 TFW/USAF

NIGHT PENETRATION was A-10A 78-0686 from the 354th TFW's 355th TFS – the only A-10 squadron in the Gulf especially trained for night missions. This example completed 60 combat sorties and is credited with destroying one Scud launcher, 5 artillery pieces, 4 tanks, 8 armored vehicles and 5 trucks. 354 TFW/USAF

Captain Terry M. Featherston cleverly included the initials of his daughter and wife – Victoria And Lynette – in the name of his aircraft: VAL'S AVENGER. This 354 TFW, 353 TFS A-10A, 78-0664, bore kill markings for one radar site, 6 artillery pieces, 4 tanks, 5 armored vehicles and 4 trucks. 354 TFW/ USAF

A-10A 79-0099, a 355 TFS "Falcons" aircraft was adorned with a stylized lion and the name FANG. This Warthog accounted for 7 artillery pieces, 10 tanks, 9 armored vehicles and 15 trucks, while completing 77 combat sorties. 354 TFW/USAF

GEORGIA GIRL was A-10A 79-0100, from the 354 TFW, 355 TFS. She is credited with 58 combat sorties and carried kill markings for one radar site, 3 artillery pieces, 3 tanks, 6 armored vehicles and 11 trucks. 354 TFW/USAF

A-10A 78-0654 KING OF PAIN, 354 TFW, 355 TFS carried this fearsome looking creature on no less than 86 combat sorties. Kills included 4 radar sites, 2 Scud launchers, 14 artillery pieces, 6 tanks, 15 armored vehicles and 10 trucks. 354 TFW/USAF

This female warrior was painted on A-10A 78-0667, INDIAN MAIDEN, from the 354 TFW, 353 TFS. Kills accumulated over 35 missions included 2 radar sites, 10 artillery pieces, 4 tanks and a truck. 354 TFW/USAF

A-10A, 78-0668, bears the legend #1 TANK KILLER, claiming more tank kills than any other 354th TFW aircraft – 27. Assigned to the 353rd TFS, this 'Hog' also dispatched 2 radar sites, 20 artillery pieces, 2 armored vehicles and 19 trucks while completing 67 combat sorties. 354th TFW/USAF

KISS OF DEATH, A-10A 78-0677, was another 354 TFW, 353 TFS jet. In the process of completing 55 combat sorties KISS OF DEATH saw to the demise of 3 radar sites, 13 artillery pieces, 8 tanks, 4 armored vehicles and 13 trucks. 354 TFW/USAF

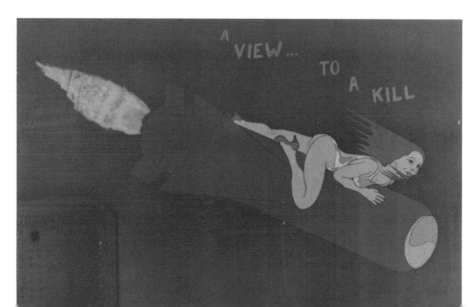

A VIEW... TO A KILL, artwork on A-10A 78-0680, 354 TFW, 353 TFS, depicts a curvy young lady wearing a "chocolate chip" desert camouflage bathing suit and riding an infra-red AGM-65 Maverick missile. A veteran of 70 combat missions, this A-10 made short work of 2 Scud launchers, 17 artillery pieces, 17 tanks, 9 armored vehicles and 22 trucks. 354 TFW/USAF

Another variation on the big gun and Warthog theme, this artwork was carried by A-10A 78-0592 of the 354 TFW, 355 TFS. Assigned to Col. Ervin "Sandy" Sharpe, BULLET EXPRESS completed 57 combat sorties. Kills consist of one Scud launcher, 4 artillery pieces, 5 tanks, 3 armored vehicles and 4 trucks. 354 TFW/USAF

TAWAKALNA DUDE..., artwork on A-10A 79-0126, 354 TFW, 353 TFS, shows Bart Simpson standing defiantly atop a Mk.20 Rockeye II cluster bomb. Bart is challenging the Tawakalna, a division of the Iraqi Republican Guard. This aircraft completed 56 combat sorties and destroyed 2 Scud launchers, 14 artillery pieces, 16 tanks, 8 armored vehicles, and 16 trucks. 354 TFW/USAF

THE FORTUNE TELLER, A-10A 78-0593, 354 TFW, 353 TFS completed 86 combat sorties during Operation Desert Storm, racking up the usual variety of Warthog kills – one Scud launcher, 10 artillery pieces, 16 tanks, 10 armored vehicles and 11 trucks. 354 TFW/USAF

The mascot of the 353rd TFS, a fierce panther, appears to be leaping from a hole torn in the side of A-10A 78-0595 RIP 'N TEAR; which claimed 4 artillery pieces, 13 tanks, 8 armored vehicles and 10 trucks over 55 missions. 354th TFW/USAF

PLAYTIME was another 354 TFW, 353 TFS A-10A, 78-0681. Though most of the 354th's aircraft carried artwork in the Gulf the majority of these unique and historic paintings were removed shortly after they returned home. PLAYTIME completed 57 combat missions and wore kill markings for 13 artillery pieces, 10 tanks, 2 armored vehicles and 7 trucks. 354 TFW/USAF

PANTHER 1 a 354 TFW A-10A (78-0715) from the 353rd TFS "Panthers" completed 68 combat missions and destroyed 12 artillery, pieces, 18 tanks 2 armored vehicles and 11 trucks. 354 TFW/USAF

The 23rd Tactical Air Support Squadron, 602nd Tactical Air Control Wing, deployed OA-10As from Davis-Monthan AFB to the Persian Gulf region in November 1990 in preparation for Desert Storm. CHRISTINE is OA-10A 77-0265 of the 23rd TASS. An Elmer Fudd-like character on the ladder door says BE VEWY, VEWY QUIET – WE'RE HUNTING IWAQIES. Wally Van Winkle

Art on OA-10A 77-0183 WILD THING, 23rd TASS, depicts a girl soaring through the night sky on the barrels of a GAU-8A. Bart, on the ladder door, is making sport of the acronym for forward air control WHAT THE FAC DUDE!. 17 nail mission marks are carried. Wally Van Winkle

ERIN O, THE LAS VEGAS OPTION is OA-10A 77-0209, also from the 23rd TASS. The 23rd's Gulf War FAC missions are represented on the planes by nail symbols applied above the battery access panel. Each nail represents three missions. Wally Van Winkle

OA-10A 76-0537, 23rd TASS, is ANGEL, BAD TO THE BONE. The art depicts a skeletal figure ripping out of the Arizona state flag, with an "Uncle Sam" hat in one hand and a nail in the other. 21 nails make up the mission tally. The wife and daughters of crew chief SSgt Gracyalny are named on the ladder door. Wally Van Winkle

LIVE AND LET DIE is carried on the nose of OA-10A 77-0200, 23rd TASS, and the door art commemorates Desert Storm with RIDERS OF THE STORM, 17 JAN-28 FEB 1991, "Nails-N-Roses" themed art incorporating family names. Under the name band 22 mission symbols are visible. Wally Van Winkle

LENNI MAY, LIVE TO FLY – FLY TO KILL is OA-10A 77-0185 of the 23rd TASS. Wally Van Winkle

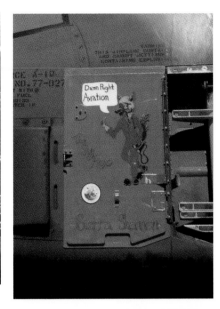

THE SLY FOX, OA-10A 77-0270 of the 23rd TASS, is assigned to Lt. Col. Jeffrey D. Fox. This jet bears a line of 16 nails from Gulf War service. Lt. Col. Fox was shot down on 19 February while flying 76-0543 and served time as a POW. Wally Van Winkle

A scantily-clad brunette glares down from the side of REGULATED TANG, OA-10A 77-0201, from the 23rd TASS. The door art features a Warthog Desert Storm cloud with the 23rd's "NF" tailcode – which stands for "Nail FAC"; Nail being the call sign the squadron used in Vietnam, and still uses today. Wally Van Winkle

PORKY'S REVENGE, with the Warner Brothers cartoon character tossing a white phosphorus target-marker rocket, is OA-10A 77-0218, 23rd TASS – marked with 22 nails. Wally Van Winkle

THE WARRIOR was painted on OA-10A 77-0186, 23rd TASS, along with 18 nails – representative of 54 sorties. On the door is THE BOX SEAT with a Warthog FAC pilot making the most of his vantage point. Wally Van Winkle

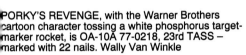

OA-10A 77-0270, MISSI LYNN, WESTERN BEAUTY!, is another 23rd TASS 'Hog with wartime experience; marked with 16 mission symbols. Wally Van Winkle

MARY JANE – with patriotic Statue of Liberty, Stars and Stripes and U.S. map artwork – is OA-10A 76-0529 of the 23rd TASS. A single nail mission symbol appears of what was surely one of the oldest 'Hogs in Desert Storm. Crew chief SSgt Brunt painted LOVELY LITA on the boarding ladder door for his wife. Wally Van Winkle

The artwork on 23rd TASS OA-10A 76-0547 THE UNKNOWN BOMBER originated in Berkeley Breathed's "Bloom County" comic strip. A Basselope – basset and antelope apparently – can be easily configured into a weapon called the "Cruise Basselope" as seen here. The door on -547 carries a six of spades and six of diamonds pierced by a white phosphorous rocket, THE 23rd DEATH CARD. A total of 22 nails are applied to this jet for FAC missions; along with kill markings for 8 tanks, 4 armored vehicles, 23 artillery pieces, 4 Scud launchers and 14 trucks destroyed while loaned to another unit and operated as a conventional A-10. This was the only 'Hog to fly both FAC and close air support/ground attack missions in the Gulf War. Wally Van Winkle

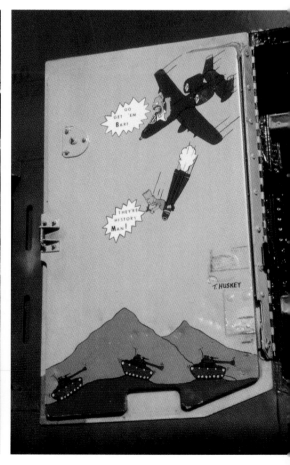

EL JEFE, DRAGON is OA-10A 77-0188 from the 22nd TASTS, 602 TACW at Davis-Monthan AFB. Wally Van Winkle

PUTT PUTT, GET OUTA MY WAY is door art on A-10A 79-0202, 357 FS, 355 FW, depicting a very warthog-like Warthog. Wally Van Winkle

Bart Simpson again, this time with his dad Homer, on a A-10A 75-0289 from the 357th FS, 355th FW, based at Davis-Monthan AFB. Wally Van Winkle

RUNNIN' WITH THE DEVIL is A-10A 75-0285 of the 355th FW, 357th FS. Wally Van Winkle

FAC U is A-10A 77-0222, 333rd FS, 355 FW. The 355th has been training A-10 combat crews since the Warthog became operational. Wally Van Winkle

A-10A 75-0291, 355 TFW, was BERT'S BEAST in 1980. Wally Van Winkle

LOW AND SLOW IS THE WAY TO GO, door art on A-10A 75-0274, depicts an A-10 with speedbrakes open cruising above the Arizona desert with the shadow of a F-117 Stealth Fighter. Wally Van Winkle

Two 'Hogs in the sunset, a fitting scene applied to A-10A 77-0224 from the 355th TTW circa 1988. Wally Van Winkle

Based on a T-shirt design, and including a small map indicating the 355 FW's home base, this art is found on A-10A 75-0222, 357 FS. Wally Van Winkle

DEATH FROM ABOVE is A-10A 77-0214, another 357 FS, 355 FW jet. Wally Van Winkle

An exotic bit of door art signed by T. Husky on A-10A 75-0281, 357 FS, 355 FW. Wally Van Winkle

Painted in the original gray scheme, A-10A 77-0181 had a stalking panther applied to the ladder door while serving in 1980 with the 354th TFW, 353rd TFS "Panthers." Wally Van Winkle

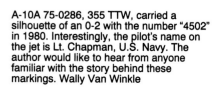

Seen here in April 1981, A-10A 76-0515 from the 355th TFW was named TAZZ – marked with both pilot and crew chief Tasmanian devils. Wally Van Winkle

Popeye appeared on SEAMAN, a well-weathered 355 TTW A-10A (75-0282), photographed on 15 June 1980. Wally Van Winkle

A-10A 75-0286, 355 TTW, carried a silhouette of an 0-2 with the number "4502" in 1980. Interestingly, the pilot's name on the jet is Lt. Chapman, U.S. Navy. The author would like to hear from anyone familiar with the story behind these markings. Wally Van Winkle

HAVE GUN WILL TRAVEL is A-10A 79-0224 from the 511th TFS, 10th TFW. The art is signed by artist J. Trago, who decorated several Alconbury A-10's for desert duty. Wally Van Winkle

Artwork inside the boarding ladder door on A-10A 79-0201, 23 TFW, attests to the fighting heritage of the famed Flying Tigers – BURMA TO BAGHDAD, from Claire Chennault's WW II American Volunteer Group to Operation Desert Storm. Walker

BAYOU BABY was A-10A 80-0177, 76 TFS, 23rd TFW, in 1989. The symbology in the strong arms of a Sergeant supporting a pair of pilots wings might represent the crew chief's job. Wally Van Winkle

OA-10A 80-0208 is now operated by the 363rd Fighter Wing's 21st Fighter Squadron. The ladder door art depicts a caricatured 'Hog (in the style of artist Hank Caruso) from the 10th TFW at Alconbury, the jet's home. The nose art on 80-0208, ANNABELLE II, represents the close ties between the U.S. and Great Britain – an appropriate theme for Gulf War art. Wally Van Winkle

From the 23rd Fighter Wing, is A-10A 80-0246 SUPER HOG, SANDY ONE. Reference is made to the "Sandy" search and rescue mission now performed by A-10s, and the art includes a SAR H-53 helicopter winching up a downed airman. Wally Van Winkle

When the 23rd TFW transitioned to A-10s, several different-shaped sharkmouths were tried before the current design was settled upon. A large mouth with an overbite was applied to 79-0186, photographed on 6 November 1981 on a transient stopover at Vance AFB, Oklahoma. Wally Van Winkle

An interesting sentiment on A-10A 79-0182, 76 TFS, 23 TFW: DON'T WRESTLE WITH A HOG...YOU'LL BOTH GET DIRTY BUT THE HOG LOVES IT. In the Warthog's domain – low and slow –few high tech fighters would fare well against it's big gun and turning ability. Wally Van Winkle

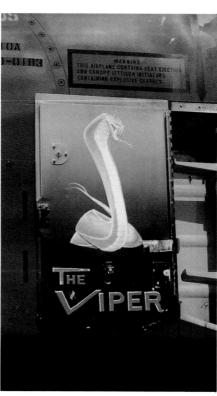

A-10A 79-0183 was THE VIPER while attached to the 23rd TFW in April 1983. Ted Paskowski via Wally Van Winkle

FROM THE ASHES A NEW BEGINNING is another Flying Tigers A-10A, 80-0201. Wally Van Winkle

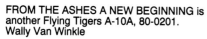

THE HUNTRESS, door art on A-10A 79-0185 of the 23rd TFW, was spotted at Nellis AFB in 1983. Ted Paskowski via Wally Van Winkle

HOG IN ARMOUR is Flying Tigers A-10A 79-0194. The ladder door well makes a handy place to temporarily store the airplane's forms. Wally Van Winkle

COOL CAT, THE LAST TIGER, A-10A 82-0665, was the last Warthog built. She was largely pieced together with spare parts at the factory, and it took a while for her first crew chief to get everything sorted out. The art is a clever adaptation of the 23rd TFW's "Flying Tiger" insignia, as seen on 80-0223. Wally Van Winkle

HOGSBREATH is A-10A 79-0184 of the 76th TFS, 23rd TFW. The doors are interchangeable, and this artwork – or a very similar piece – was carried on 79-0173 a few years before. Wally Van Winkle

WHEN PIGS FLY on A-10A 79-0210, 23rd TFW, 74th TFS, a humorous take on the "Warthog" nickname. Wally Van Winkle

Gulf War art and graffiti on a 23 TFW A-10A named MISFIT. Ground crews at forward operating locations (FOLs) would communicate back and forth by writing inside various access panels on the jets. Someone was also keeping track of combat kills on this door. USAF/SSgt Robert V. Pease

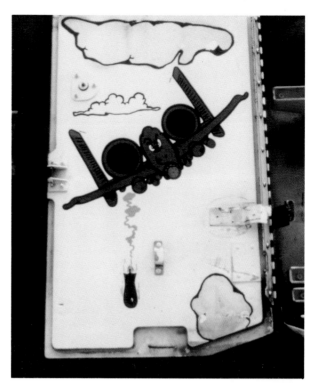

A-10A 79-0197, 23 TFW, carries an unnamed caricature that exaggerates some of the Warthog's most striking features; the big, high-mounted turbofan engines and old-fashioned looking twin tails. USAF/SSgt Robert V. Pease

A-101A 79-0177, a 23rd TFW "Flying Tigers" Warthog bears the legend LOVE MY MOOSE inside the ladder door. Paul Bigelow

LIVE FREE OR DIE was 23 TFW A-10A 80-0166. Now the 23rd Wing, the Flying Tigers have transferred from England AFB in Louisiana to Pope AFB, N.C. USAF/SSgt Robert V. Pease

A-10A 79-0213 THE HEARTBEAT OF AMERICA belonged to the 23rd TFW in 1991. USAF/SSgt Robert V.Pease

A-10A 80-0163 WE GIVE NO QUARTER is a 76th TFS, 23rd TFW machine. Wally Van Winkle

NIGHT OWL, FOREVER VIGILANT is 10A 79-0205, a 23rd TFW Desert Storm veteran Hog. Wally Van Winkle

A-10A 79-0223, 23 TFW, carried this door art LIZARD, prior to becoming the wing commander's jet with the obligatory name change to "Tiger 1." USAF/SSgt Robert V. Pease

The "Hell's Angel" served as insignia for an American Volunteer Group "Flying Tigers" P-40 squadron in China during the early days of WW II. She re-appeared on the fuselage of several 23rd TFW A-10's deployed for Desert Shield and Storm a half-century later. This 'Hog also utilized the design for ladder door art. USAF/SSgt Robert V. Pease

Door art on A-10A 79-0186, 23 TFW, represented a view of a doomed tank through the Hog's Heads Up Display. USAF/SSgt Robert V. Pease

A salivating Warthog glares from this 23rd TFW A-10A. USAF/SSgt Robert V. Pease

These markings on A-10A 80-0155, 81 TFW, represent the Warthog's chance meeting with four seagulls while taking off. The final score was 'Hog 4, seagulls 0. Paul Bigelow

The first pre-production A-10, 73-1664, carried on testing long after the 'Hog became operational; being converted into the two-seat Night/Adverse Weather demonstrator by Fairchild in 1978-79. The Air Force opted not to buy any Night 'Hogs, though the three-year evaluation program proved the N/AW A-10 to be very capable. This Owl, with "FLIR" and "Laser" eyes, was painted onto 73-1664 in May of 1979. Wally Van Winkle

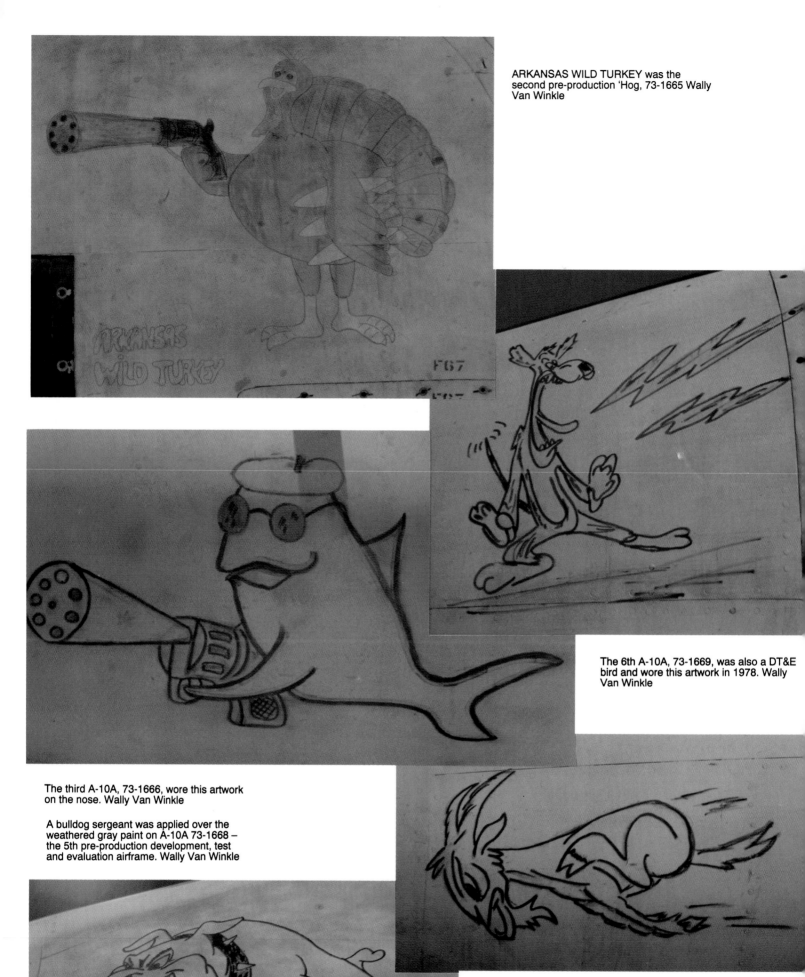

ARKANSAS WILD TURKEY was the second pre-production 'Hog, 73-1665 Wally Van Winkle

The 6th A-10A, 73-1669, was also a DT&E bird and wore this artwork in 1978. Wally Van Winkle

The third A-10A, 73-1666, wore this artwork on the nose. Wally Van Winkle

A bulldog sergeant was applied over the weathered gray paint on A-10A 73-1668 – the 5th pre-production development, test and evaluation airframe. Wally Van Winkle

A-10A number 4, 73-1667, had this charging mountain goat applied to the nose with magic marker. Wally Van Winkle

An eagle brandishing a Thompson submachine gun was applied to A-10A 81-0979, the 10th Tactical Fighter Wing Commander's personal jet, in 1990. Paul Bigelow

DARLIN' DEB, a nice piece of airbrush ladder door art, appears on A-10A 81-0951, of the 81st TFW at RAF Bentwaters. Paul Bigelow

PARTY TIME AT THE BISTRO appears on A-10A 81-0978, 78th TFS, 10th TFW. One side effect of painting artwork on the inside of the boarding ladder door is a certain degree of protection from the elements; this example having already survived for two years when photographed on April 25th 1990 at RAF Woodbridge. Also, when the door is closed no non-standard markings are visible – satisfying those who want to maintain a very uniform appearance on the ramp. Paul Bigelow

A-10A 80-0229 MEMPHIS BELLE III was operated by the 10th TFW, 511th TFS during the Gulf War. The 10th TFW deployed their Warthogs from RAF Alconbury to King Fahd Airport in Saudi Arabia. Jim Dunn

Ladder door art on A-10A 82-0655, PARTNERS IN PEACE, VICTORS IN WAR, depicts clasped American and British hands above the Warthog in flight. N. Donald

69

GIV 'EM HELL is A-10A 81-0953 of the 10th TFW, 511 TFS. Jim Dunn

NINJA is 81st TFW A-10A 80-0204. Paul Bigelow

Unnamed ladder door art on A-10A 80-0206, 81st TFW. Not surprisingly Warthogs are frequently found in A-10 artwork, as are attractive females. Paul Bigelow

Art on A-10A 80-0171, 81st TFW, features a familiar warrior, riding what would appear to be a Russian bear. Paul Bigelow

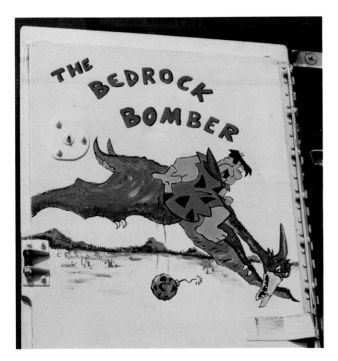

THE BEDROCK BOMBER is 81st TFW A-10A 81-0962. Paul Bigelow

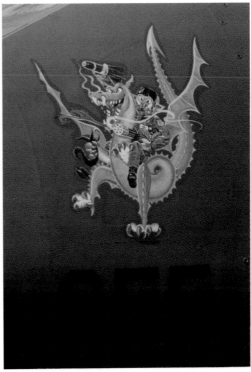

This imaginative piece of nose art, painted by aviation artist Geoff Pleasance, adorns A-10A 82-0655 – personal aircraft of 81st TFW Commander Col. Roger Radcliffe. The English griffin was taken from the 81 TFW insignia, and a Warthog pilot armed with Maverick and GAU-8A cannon completes the effect. N. Donald

Artwork virtually identical to that on 82-0655 was previously carried on A-10A 80-0181 also from the 81st TFW. Paul Bigelow

NEXT calls the executioner as pieces of tanks lie scattered about in this door art on A-10A 80-0158 of the 81st TFW. Paul Bigelow

WAR PIG was A-10A 81-0990 from the 10th TFW based at RAF Alconbury. The 10th was deactivated during the summer of 1992. Paul Bigelow

Ominous artwo
on A-10A 81-0
81 TFW, depict
the Devil himse
killing a tank. T
name UNDER
BLOOD RED S
comes from the
of a song by the
Irish rock group
2. Paul Bigelow

HEAT SEEKER appeared on A-10A 80-0236, 81st TFW, in 1990.
Paul Bigelow

DEATH FROM ABOVE, Heavy Metal inspired door art on A-10A
80-0147 of the 81st TFW, based at RAF Bentwaters. Paul
Bigelow

A Disney chara
that has turned
on numerous
aircraft since hi
screen debut in
1942, THUMPE
seen here on A
10A 81-0962 fr
the 81st TFW. I
Bigelow

A-10A 81-0944 of the 81st TFW carried this exotic bit of ladder door art entitled COSMIC STORM in 1989. Paul Bigelow

Door art on A-10A 81-0982 FREEDOM FIGHTER, 81 TFW, depicts an American eagle diving to attack with a TV-guided Maverick missile and the 'Hog's big gun. Paul Bigelow

JUSTICE FOR ALL appears on 81st TFW A-10A 81-0960. Paul Bigelow

Door art on A-10A 82-0655, 81 TFW, features Garfield the cat aboard a caricature A-10, shooting missiles at Odie. Paul Bigelow

A-10A 80-0229 also carries artwork inside the ladder door, BARTHAWG, with Bart Simpson spouting one of his trademark witticisms. This aircraft is now assigned to the 507th Air Control Wing at Shaw AFB. Jim Dunn

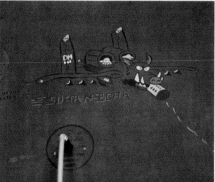

Believed to be the second regular pro
tion Warthog with external artwork 37
TFS, 355 TFW A-10A 78-0668 SOAF
BOAR carried a caricature A-10 on b
sides of the nose in 1980. The ladder
wasn't ignored either. Wally Van Win

Ladder door art on A-10A 80-0207, HEAD HUNTER, from the
81st TFW. Jim Dunn

Bart Simpson makes a
statement that many can
relate to on A-10A 80-0200,
57 FWW, SHIT HAPPENS
WHEN YOU'RE TDY! Wally
Van Winkle

ARMOR EATER, 75-0297, was probably the first A-10 assigned to a fighter unit to carry artwork on the outside
of the jet. Photographed at NAS Lemoore on 4 June 1979, ARMOR EATER was flown by the 57thFWW
out of Nellis AFB, Nevada. R. R. Burgess via Wally Van Winkle

A popular 'Hog-art subject is reprised on A-10A 80-0225 from the 57th Fighter Weapons Wing. Wally Van Winkle

The 172nd Fighter Squadron, 110th Fighter Group, Michigan ANG now flies Warthogs, replacing the OA-37B. OA-10A 81-0975 carries this art on the ladder door. Wally Van Winkle

A patriotic eagle-and-flag motif is found on OA-10A 80-0268, Michigan ANG. Wally Van Winkle

A-10A 76-0535 434 TFW, AFRES, was GENTLEMAN'S DELIGHT in 1988. Wally Van Winkle

Indiana ANG A-10A 77-0244 was named BOOMER. Again we see the "Warthog and gun" theme, which is very popular for obvious reasons. Wally Van Winkle

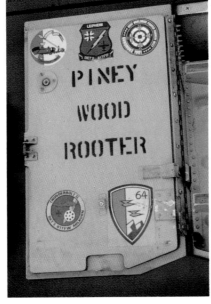

PINEY WOOD ROOTER is A-10A 79-0142, from the 915th TFW, AFRES, at Barksdale AFB, Louisiana. The door carries a brace of zaps, including that of HTG 64 – a Luftwaffe UH-I Huey wing. Wally Van Winkle

OA-10A 81-0981, GAU-8 TERMINATOR, is operated by the 111th TASG, 103rd TASS, PA ANG. The 103rd traded up to OA-10As from OA-37Bs recently. Wally Van Winkle

The New York ANG also operated A-10A 78-0707, HOGS IN SPACE. Currently the 174th TFW is equipped with F-16As dedicated to the close air support mission. Wally Van Winkle

FLYIN' RAZORBACK, A-10A 78-0671, belonged to the 174th TFG, 138th TFS, New York ANG, in 1982. Wally Van Winkle

Door art, circa 1981, on 175th TFG, 104th TFS Maryland ANG A-10A 78-0705 consists of a flying turtle armed with a GAU-8A gun and bombs. Wally Van Winkle

A-10A 78-0658 from the 174th TFW, NY ANG, was named BOSS HOGG, with artwork featuring the Dukes of Hazzard TV show character of the same name seated in the 'Hog's cockpit. Wally Van Winkle

Marvel Comic's Incredible Hulk is the subject of THE BEAST...AGAIN on A-10A 78-0706 from the 128th TFW, 167th TFS, Wisconsin ANG. Wally Van Winkle

A-10A 78-0682 of the 175th TFG, 104th TFS, Maryland ANG carries the Maryland state flag on the inside of the ladder door. Paul Bigelow

Also with the 174th TFG, SATAN'S REVENGE was A-10A 78-0670. Wally Van Winkle

A-10A 79-0195 was named THE BEAST in 1984. Wally Van Winkle

THE HOBBIT was a A-10A 76-0533, 358 TFTS, 355 TTW. Wally Van Winkle

CITY OF WESTFIELD is A-10A 79-0104 of the 104th TFG, 131st TFS, based at Barnes Municipal Airport in Westfield, Massachusetts. Wally Van Winkle

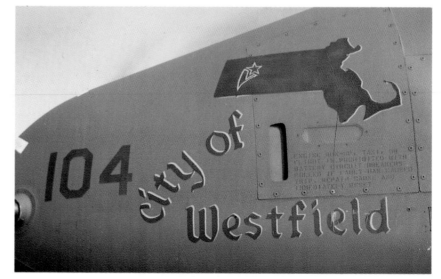

A-10A 77-0245 SWEET LADY, from the 45 FS, 930th FG, carried this door art painted by Jeff Dalton. Originally the Lady was holding two .45s; but the artwork was damaged and had to be retouched, omitting one pistol. The door was removed from the aircraft and is now on display in the museum at McClellan AFB. Jim Dunn

A couple strolling on the beach at sundown is the subject of SUNSET SPLENDOR, door art on A-10A 77-0239 from the 390th TFG, 45th TFS at Grissom AFB. Paul Bigelow

Door art on an unidentified A-10A HOGWASH shows Miss Piggy doing just that. Wally Van Winkle

THE HOGSTER PIGS OUT is a Wisconsin ANG A-10A, home based at Truax Field, north of Madison. Bob Shane

The door art on this 128th FW, Wisconsin ANG A-10A is self-explanatory. Bob Shane

A-10A 78-0605 of the 442nd TFW, 303rd TFS (AFRES) carried this artwork KC HAWGS in 1990. Based at Richards-Gebaur AFB, south of Kansas City, Missouri, the 442nd's Warthogs wear the tail code "KC." Paul Bigelow

Another 128 FW A-10A is DESERT THUNDER. Bob Shane

A-10A 77-0184, another AFRES 'Hog with the 45th TFS was named BATTLIN' BADGER. Paul Bigelow

Signed by artist J. Trago, the Gulf War art on A-10A 79-0220 YANKEE EXPRESS of the 10th TFW, 511th TFS gets the point across. Bob Shane

THE GREAT AMERICAN HOG

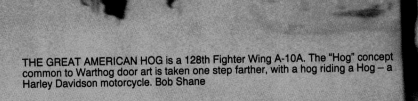

THE GREAT AMERICAN HOG is a 128th Fighter Wing A-10A. The "Hog" concept common to Warthog door art is taken one step farther, with a hog riding a Hog – a Harley Davidson motorcycle. Bob Shane

CHAPTER 7
F-16 FIGHTING FALCON

F-16C 83-1159, 363 TFW, 17 TFS, carried the Batman logo – the "Batsign." Mission symbols are applied to both sides of the fuselage below the canopy, the "Batjet" having flown 45 sorties.
Michael J. Hrivnak, 363 FW

SSgt Warren D. Trask applied some very fine artwork to a handful of the F-16s deployed from the 363rd TFW at Shaw AFB, to Al Dafra Air Base, Sharjah, United Arab Emirates during the Gulf War. F-16C 85-1419, the wing commander's aircraft, carried this insignia. The attacking falcon is representative of the F-16 Falcon and the 33rd TFS "Falcons." The pyramid represents stability in the region, and the shooting star honors Wing Commander Col. Ralph E. Eberhart, and his promotion to Brigadier General.
Michael J. Hrivnak, 363 FW

The painting "Vampire's Kiss" by fantasy artist Boris Vallejo inspired this nose art on NIGHT STALKER, F-16C 84-1256, 363 TFW, 17 TFS. This jet flew 28 bombing missions in the Gulf. Michael J. Hrivnak, 363 FW

"CODE-ONE" CANDY was Trask's first piece of nose art, applied to F-16C 85-1420, 363 TFW, 33 TFS. "Code one", generally referring to an aircraft, means in perfect operating condition or 100% capable. This jet flew 56 missions in Operation Desert Storm. Michael J. Hrivnak, 363 FW

Another piece of art by Trask, MAX THRUST appeared on F-16C 83-1150, 363 TFW, 33 TFS, a 50-mission veteran. Unfortunately, all of the artwork was removed shortly after the 363rd's aircraft returned home. Michael J. Hrivnak, 363 FW

Trask's tribute to the 19th AMU "Game-cocks", who deployed in support of the 363rd TFW, HOT COCK appeared on 33rd TFS F-16C 84-1219. A "cocked" aircraft is on alert for a quick start-up, and the term "hot cocked" means engine run-up has been completed, all systems are in the green and the aircraft is ready for launch. David F. Brown

HAMMER TIME, F-16C 84-1281, 363 TFW, 33 TFS, flew 46 missions. A female security police officer, Jackhammer Jenny, riding a bomb is a nice variation on the Dr. Strangelove idea. Michael J. Hrivnak, 363rd FW

F-16C 83-1158, 363 TFW, 33 TFS, was named SWEET...BUT DEADLY!. The artwork depicts a woman with a scorpion's tail crawling through what appears to be a jagged hole in the side of the aircraft. SWEET...BUT DEADLY completed 47 missions.
Michael J. Hrivnak, 363 FW

HOOTER'S STAN-DARDS was F-16C 84-1241 from the 17th TFS "Hooters", 363 TFW, with 46 missions to her credit. Michael J. Hrivnak, 363 FW

WAR WENCH F-16C 84-1247, 363 TFW, 17 TFS, racked up 37 missions before the cease-fire on 28 February 1991. Michael J. Hrivnak, 363 FW

HARMFUL F/X was F-16C 83-1142, 363 TFW, 33 TFS. This aircraft flew 42 missions alongside the other Shaw F-16s under the 363rd Tactical Fighter Wing (Provisional). Michael J. Hrivnak, 363 FW

Bart Simpson takes a shot at Saddam. EAT MY SHORTS HUSSEIN is F-16C 84-1244, 363 TFW, 17 TFS, a 56 mission veteran. David F. Brown

This owl was applied to F-16C 84-1217, flown by the commander of the 17th TFS "Hooters" squadron, 363 TFW. 84-1217 completed 39 missions. Michael J. Hrivnak, 363 FW

HERE, HUSSEIN, SURPRISE!!! on F-16C 83-1165 of the 363 TFW, 17 TFS, with 42 sorties. David F. Brown

After 49 missions against Iraqi targets, F-16C 84-1223, 363 TFW, 17 TFS, is proclaimed to be HUSSEIN'S WORST NIGHTMARE David F. Brown

"Spaceman Spiff", alter-ego of Calvin from the Calvin And Hobbes comic strip, opens fire in this artwork on WILD CHILD, F-16C 84-1265. From the 363 TFW, 33 TFS, this aircraft flew 43 missions. Michael J. Hrivnak, 363 FW

A gangling jester, WILD THANG was applied to F-16C 84-1240, a 363 TFW, 33 TFS bird credited with 46 missions. Michael J. Hrivnak, 363 FW

F-16C 84-1260 THE BARBARIAN, 184 FG, Kansas ANG. Artwork by Kevin Tomlin. With the entire gear door painted, THE BARBARIAN is very easy to distinguish from other aircraft in the pattern overhead. Walker

The Tasmanian Devil went to war on F-16C 84-1213 of the 363 TFW, 17 TFS and completed 47 bombing missions. Though here Taz is equipped with an AIM-9 Sidewinder, F-16s were employed primarily in an air-to-ground role during the Gulf War. Michael J. Hrivnak, 363 FW

NEXT on F-16C 84-1254, 363 TFW, 17 TFS. This aircraft completed 38 missions. Michael J. Hrivnak, 363FW

BLOOD STORM, F-16C 84-1261, 363 TFW, 17 TFS, flew 40 missions carrying this artwork; an armored desert warrior brandishing two scimitars. Michael J. Hrivnak, 363 FW

F-16C 84-1315 SABRE ONE returned home to the 50th TFW at Hahn AB decorated with this knight in gleaming chrome armor. The 50th TFW deployed two dozen block-25 F-16Cs from the 10th TFS to become part of the 363rd TFW (P) at Al Dafra during Desert Shield/Storm. Paul Bigelow

ACES HIGH, artwork inspired by an album cover from the heavy metal group Iron Maiden, decorates F-16C 84-1376, 184th FG. 84-1376 deployed for Operation Desert Storm with the 50th TFW, 10 TFS. Walker

The nose art on 184th FG F-16C 83-1183 WINSTON CUP SERIES would seem to indicate that the crew chief is a fan of NASCAR racing, with the number "17" showing support for driver Darrell Waltrip. Walker

THE REBEL is F-16C 83-1137, from the 184th FG. Walker

DESERT FOX is F-16C 83-1144 of the 184 FG. This jet belonged to the 363 TFW, 33 TFS at the time of the Gulf War, and carries 54 mission symbols. Walker

A curious combination of F-16 and all terrain vehicle is the subject of the nose art on F-16C 84-1250 TAKE IT OUT AND PLAY WITH IT of the 184th FG. Walker

Crew chief Steve Domingues, a drag racer and Chevrolet enthusiast, named his 184th FG F-16D, 83-1182, THE HEARTBEAT OF KANSAS. Walker

VIPER DRIVER, painted by Bob Johnston, enjoyed a brief existance on a 184th TFG F-16C 84-1385. The art was done for pilot Kasey "Viper" Carlson's retirement. The jet's crew chief was Brad Beyer. "Viper" is also an unofficial name for the F-16, preferred by most over "Fighting Falcon." Bob Johnston

Richard Dudley painted the nose art on TOTALLY AWESOME, F-16C 84-1386 of the 184th FG. Walker

MEYER FLYER, an excellent rendering of Vargas' December 1943 Esquire pin-up, was applied to crew chief Gordon Meyer's F-16C (83-1148) by Bob Johnston as a wedding gift. Sadly, the order came to remove the door art from all the unit's jets at virtually the same time. MEYER FLYER was gone before the honeymoon was over. Bob Johnston

"STEADY" AS SHE GOES MATE is F-16C 84-1222, 184 FG. The pilot, and ex-Navy flier whose call sign is "Steady", wanted the Cracker Jack kid on the airplane. Crew chief Newell Applegate was agreeable and suggested the American flag be added. Walker

F-16C 84-1265, WILD CHILD during the Gulf War, now belongs to the 184th FG and carries these mission symbols. It is reported that some mission tallys are confused by the fact that aircraft would fly a mission and recover at a different base, then launch on another sortie from that location on the way back. Walker

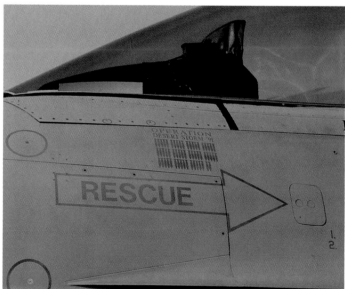

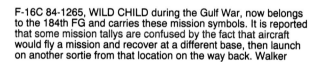

MEYER FLYER being unceremoniously sanded off. Bob Johnston

As a joke, this sketch, THE AUCTIONEER, was applied to F-16D 84-1396 when her crew chief was studying to be an auctioneer. The 184th FG is tasked with the training of new F-16 pilots, and is therefore assigned an unusually large proportion of two-seaters. Walker

The artwork on this 184th FG F-16D, 84-1325 AMERICAN MUSCLE, NEXT..., was at least partially inspired by the art applied to F-16C 84-1254 during the Gulf War. Walker

Also from the 184th FG, F-16C 84-1258 is a dog, despite the efforts of a conscientious crew chief who keeps the aircraft in pristine condition. Missles won't fire, bombs invariably go long. Somebody wondered what would happen if they hung a travel pod on the aircraft and this bit of artwork, PODS LONG, sketched on the nose gear door by Bob Johnston, was born. Walker

HIGH FIDELITY, DON'T TREAD ON ME is another 184th FG F-16C, 83-1136. Walker

IF YOU CAN'T PARTY WITH THE BIG BOYS DON'T SHOW UP! is F-16D 83-1181 from the 184th FG, Kansas ANG. Walker

CITY OF KLAMATH FALLS is F-16A 82-1014, the 114th Tactical Fighter Training Squadron's "tail bird." Operating out of Kingsley Field, near Klamath Falls, Oregon, the 114th provides air defense training for all ANG units flying the air defense F-16 mission. Jim Dunn

F-16C 84-1279 of the 184th FG was named MATO PO TAN'KA –Sioux for "Bear With A Loud Voice." This is the second F-16 crewed by TSgt Shawn Henderson-who puts "Lips" in some form on all of his jets, hence the small Roman numeral and pair of lips. MATO PO TAN'KA was the last Jayhawk door art to be removed. Walker

LITTLE PRECIOUS, SWEET SIXTEEN! is F-16A 79-0402, utilized for test duties by the Ogden Air Logistic Center at Hill AFB, Utah, which handles depot-level maintenance on the F-16 fleet. The jet wears a high-conspicuity red and white paint scheme with the artwork applied to the left ventral fin. N. Donald

F-16A 79-0377 CITY OF YOUNGSTOWN, carries on the 906th FG tradition of naming their jets after cities in Ohio. Walker

Along the upper fuselage of F-16A 81-0675, 125 FIG, is a combination of a falcon's head and the lightning bolt normally carried on the tail of the Florida ANG aircraft. Wally Van Winkle

Seen at Red Flag in March 1987, F-16A 83-1079 from the 401st TFW, 613th TFS, wears the name FLAK RAT below the radar warning receiver on the nose. Then based at Torrejon AB, near Milan, the 401st was asked to vacate Spanish territory and was to be moved to Crotone, Italy, but fell victim to the current force reductions and was disbanded. Wally Van Winkle

F-16C 85-1552 from the 192nd TFG, Virginia ANG, is BEAR NECESSITIES This was the first and only Virginia Viper to receive nose art, as word came late in 1992 that artwork would no longer be allowed on the Guard F-16s. Don Logan

HANDY STITCH was 184th FG-16C 83-1137; named for the pilot, who's nickname is "Stitch." Bob Johnston

CHAPTER 8
A-7D/K CORSAIR II

Flamboyant markings on the 180th TFG "Stings" tail bird, A-7D 72-0180. Based at Toledo, the Ohio ANG 180th Fighter Group transitioned to the F-16C in Spring of 1992. Bob Shane

A-7D 72-0235 from the 156th Fighter Group "Bucaneros" (Buccaneers) wore this artwork marking the end of an era, as the Puerto Rico ANG relinquished their faithful A-7s after 17 years in favor of F-16As. Bob Shane

A-7D 71-0345 was named MIGHTY MOUSE and carried the appropriate artwork while assigned to the 127th TFG, Michigan ANG in 1988. Jim Meehan

A-7D 72-0228 SERGEANT AT ARMS, 192 TFG, was the personal mount of Maj. Randy Hamel. Jim Meehan via Bob Dorsey

SASSY SUSIE was Maj. Dave Dornan's 192 TFG A-7D, 70-0955. The aircraft was transferred to the 121st TFW in November 1991. Jim Meehan via Bob Dorsey

Seen here at Richmond in 1988, A-7D 71-0364 of the 192nd TFG, 149th TFS Virginia ANG was named THE GAMBLER by Capt. Garry Drummond. The A-7D/K is out of active duty service with the Air Force and the Air National Guard units are gradually trading in their SLUFs for more modern hardware. Virginia has transitioned to the GE F-110 powered F-16C. Jim Meehan via L. N. Paul

CORS-HARE II, a clever play on words, was found on 192 TFG A-7D 70-0943; flown by Maj. Barry Mountcastle. Though the Air Force never officially adopted the Navy's name for the A-7, Corsair II, it is often used — alongside other epithets such as SLUF — when referring to A-7s from both services. Jim Meehan via Bob Dorsey

THE PLAYMATE, one in a series of "Playmate" pin-ups applied to Maj. Glenn Morton's A-7D, 71-0350, 192 TFG, Virginia ANG. This version appeared in 1985. Jim Meehan via Bob Dorsey

DEATH DEALER was A-7D 70-0966 assigned to Lt. Col. Roger Legg, 192 TFG, VA ANG. The jet was retired in October 1991. Jim Meehan via Bob Dorsey

The artwork on Virginia ANG A-7D 71-0371 PANAMA EXPRESS reflected a favorite TDY of Maj. Taylor Cole and a fondness for the beer found there. Jim Meehan via Bob Dorsey

The final 192nd TFW artwork applied to A-7D 71-0371, a variation on the same theme, photographed at AMARC in the fall of 1991. Jerry Fugere

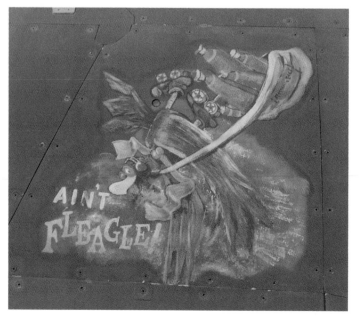

REBEL RIDER was the 192nd TFG's single two-seat A-7K, 80-0288 assigned to Lt. Col. Bill Rose and Col. Dave Hudson. The artwork depicted a charging line of Confederate soldiers. One of only 31 two-seat combat-capable trainer K-models produced, REBEL RIDER was retired in October 1991. The Virginia ANG's emblem which includes the Confederate battle flag, was also recently retired to avoid upsetting those who find that era in the heritage of the Virginia Militia offensive. Jim Meehan via Bob Dorsey

After F-105D 61-0145 "My Honeypot" was retired, came A-7D 69-6197 HONEY POT 2, 192 TFG, Virginia ANG. Paul Bigelow

AIN'T FLEAGLE was another 192 TFG, Virginia ANG A-7D, 71-0333. Jim Meehan

This Virginia ANG A-7D, 75-0386 RED DOG LEADER, was assigned to Lt. Col. (then Major) Roger Legg when photographed in October 1982. At that time the 192nd TFG's A-7s were painted in the wrap-around tan and green camouflage that preceeded today's two-tone gray scheme. L. N. Paul

VIRGINIA GENTLEMAN is A-7D 70-0979 of the 192 TFG, Virginia ANG. Assigned to Lt. Col. Don Everett, the airplane was named after a brand of bourbon whiskey. Paul Bigelow

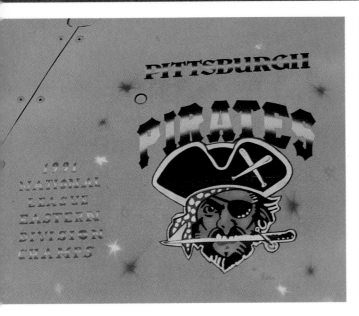

A-7D 71-0362 of the 112th TFG, 146th TFS home based at Greater Pittsburgh IAP, honored the 1991 National League East Champion PITTSBURGH PIRATES with this bit of panel art. Paul Bigelow

Not to be left out, the 1991 Stanley Cup Champion PITTSBURGH PENGUINS were represented on A-7D 73-0997, 112th TFG. The unit is now the 112th Air Refueling Wing, having swapped A-7s for KC-135Es. Paul Bigelow

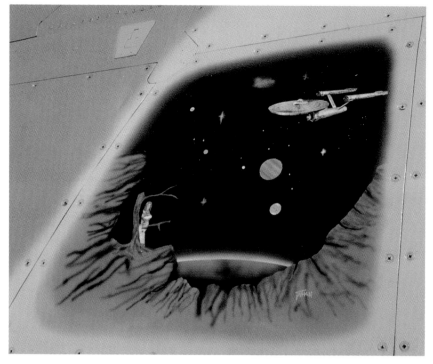

A-7D 72-0227, 127 TFW, Michigan ANG, was named HOT STUFF in 1988. Wally Van Winkle

An interesting little piece of artwork can be seen on SINBAD, A-7D 71-0294 from the 121st TFW, Ohio ANG at Rickenbacker ANGB. Wally Van Winkle

Considering the immense popularity of all things Star Trek, the artwork on Pennsylvania ANG, A-7D 72-0194, 112 TFG, seems logical. Wally Van Winkle

A handful of 132 TFW, 124 TFS, Iowa ANG A-7's had artwork applied to the inside of a main landing gear door. CASPER, THE GREY GHOST, alongside the 124th's "Ugly ... but well hung" zap, was found on A-7D 70-0138. Wally Van Winkle

A-7D 69-6222 of the 162 TFS, 178 TFG, Ohio ANG, is named SCRAPPY after a P-51 Mustang that served with the unit's ancestral WWII group. Paul Bigelow

A little bird and a bottle of "241 proof" adorn A-7D 72-0241, HAPPY HOUR FOUR, 132 TFW, Iowa ANG. Wally Van Winkle

The personal jet of Col. "Lance" Meyer, CITY OF SPRING-FIELD is A-7D 72-0178; from the 178th TFG, based at Capitol Airport just north of Springfield, Ohio. Wally Van Winkle

A-7D 72-0215, 132 TFW, carried this caricature on the gear door. The Iowa Guard at Des Moines has recently transitioned to F-16Cs. Wally Van Winkle

A-7D 69-6192 CITY OF WALTERS was captured on film at Sheppard in 1983. For a time, Aircraft utilized as ground training airframes at the Sheppard TTC were named after nearby towns. Paul Bigelow

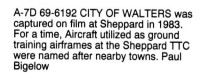

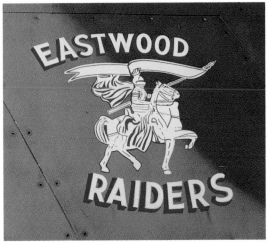

CITY OF HENRIETTA was A-7D 69-6196, last flown by the 23rd TFW "Flying Tigers". The 23rd operated A-7Ds from 1972 until 1980 when it began accepting A-10A Warthogs. The aircraft was photograped at Sheppard AFB, Texas, in 1983, in use as a training airframe. Paul Bigelow

EASTWOOD RAIDERS is A-7D 70-0937, 185 TFG. Wally Van Winkle

A-7D 69-6203, 185 TFG, is BOYDEN-HULL COMETS. Wally Van Winkle

The Sioux City — based A-7s of the 185th TFG, 174th TFS, Iowa ANG, wore the colors of area high schools prior to their retirement. A-7D 69-6210 was named for the UNITY CHRISTIAN KNIGHTS. Bob Shane

WESTWOOD REBELS is A-7D 69-6193, 185th TFG. The A-7 served with the 185th from 1976 to 1992. Bob Shane

The 185th TFG's two-seat SLUF, A-7K 81-0073 is WEST HIGH WOLVERINES. Wally Van Winkle

KINGSLEY-PIERSON PANTHERS, A-7D 75-0406, 185 TFG. Wally Van Winkle

95

SOUTH SIOUX CITY CARDINALS is another 185th TFG Iowa ANG A-7D. Bob Shane

Iowa ANG A-7D 75-0405 carries the mascot of the LAWTON-BRONSON EAGLES. The 185th TFG flew close air support in Vietnam from Phu Cat AB in 1968 and 69 with F-l00 Super Sabres. Bob Shane

LEMARS COMMUNITY BULLDOGS is A-7D 72-0182, 185 TFG. Bob Shane

WOODBURY CENTRAL WILDCATS appears beside the 185th TFG emblem on A-7D 71-0358. Wally Van Winkle

A-7D 69-6215, 185th, also carries the name and mascot of a local school: NORTH HIGH STARS. Bob Shane

AKRON-WESTFIELD WESTERNERS was another 185 TFG A-7D. Wally Van Winkle

CHAPTER 9

F-15 EAGLE

F-15C 85-0114 of the 33rd TFW, 58 TFS wears two green stars and two Iraqi flags, one of each for her MiG kills. Captain Cesar A. Rodriguez was at the controls of -114 for both victories. The first kill came on 19 January 1991 when a MiG 29 flew into the ground while maneuvering to escape; the second kill was made on 26 January – Capt. Rodriguez downing a MiG 23 with an AIM-7 Sparrow missile. The F-15s mastery of the skies over Iraq, plus the quickness of hostile aircraft to run from the F-14s powerful radar (which they knew well from the Iran-Iraq war) could account for the Tomcat scoring only one Gulf War aerial victory. David F. Brown

F-15C 85-0102 GULF SPIRIT is one of three 33 TFW Eagles (one from each squadron) to carry the name, which was also used when the wing flew F-15As. The Gulf referred to is the Gulf of Mexico rather than the Persian Gulf, but the 33rd scored 17 of the 41 aerial victories of Desert Storm while deployed to Tabuk, Saudi Arabia. The green star represents Col. Rick Parson's downing of two Su-22s on 7 February 1991 while flying aircraft 85-0124. The Iraqi flags mark Capt. David G. Rose's victory over a MiG 23 while flying -102 on 29 January and Capt Anthony R. Murphy's destruction of two Su-22s in -102 on 7 February. The AIM-7 was the weapon of choice in all of these engagements. David F. Brown

The green star on F-15C 83-0017 represents the downing of an Iraqi Mirage F1 near Baghdad on 17 January 1991 by Captain Steven Tate of the 1st TFW, 71st TFS; using an AIM-7M Sparrow missile. This was the first official aerial victory of the Gulf War, and the 1st TFW's only kill. Walker

F-15C 84-0021 of the 53rd TFS, 36 TFW at Bitburg AB, Germany, was given this striking tiger-stripe paint job for the 1991 Tiger Meet. Paul Bigelow

F-15A 75-0036, wearing the short-lived light blue paint scheme early F-15s were delivered in, was named THE TIDEWATER ALLIGATOR while serving with the 1st TFW in the late 1970's. The name of then-TAC Commander General Robert J. Dixon was also painted on the aircraft. Jim Meehan

SPIRIT OF THE VIRGINIA PENINSULA, the name found on this F-15A (74-0117) photographed at Langley on 14 July 1992 – possibly intended for static display – was simultaneously carried by active 1st FW F-15C 83-0033. Jim Meehan

F-15A 74-0083, 1 TFW, was named PENINSULA PATRIOT in the Spring of 1976. Jim Meehan

The extent of personalized markings on 85th Test & Evaluation Squadron aircraft is seen on F-15C 85-0126 GUNNY'S GAL, and F-15C 84-0011 THE TERMINATOR. The 85th TES performs varied testing duties out of the Tactical Air Warfare Center at Eglin AFB, Florida. Walker

F-15A 76-0071, another 1st TFW jet, bore a depiction of the Liberty Bell and the name PHILADELPHIA FREEDOM in 1981. Jim Meeham

It is said that the 1st FW has kept the name MALONEY'S PONY on one of their aircraft since World War II, when it orginated on Thomas Maloney's 1st Fighter Group P-38. The latest incarnation appears on F-15C 82-0023, belonging to the 27th FS, 1st FW – the first operational squadron to fly F-15s. Jim Meehan

CHAPTER 10
USAF F-4 PHANTOM II

F-4E 67-0351 was named SPIRIT OF FREEDOM while operated by the 497th TFS, 51st Composite Wing at Taegu in 1986. A Pave Spike laser designator is carried in the left forward AIM-7 well, along with a single AIM-9 Sidewinder and tiny practice bombs on the inboard wing pylons. The "GU" Phantoms were eventually turned over to the Republic of Korea Air Force. Wally Van Winkle

F-4E 68-0370 wore the unit-wide 108th TFW Princeton Tiger nose markings along with the name BINGO'S BABY. This Phantom went straight from the New Jersey Air National Guard to the Republic of Korea Air Force when the 108th transitioned to KC-135Es in 1991. via Rene Francillon

MALONES MAGNUM is F-4E 66-0357 (as in .357 Magnum) from the 108th TFW, NJANG. The name appears on the gun fairing. Someone apparently added the word "drone" to the name, after learning the F-4Es will be converted into aerial targets when the supply of F-106s is exhausted. via Rene Francillon

RAT BOY'S RATMOBILE was F-4E 68-0358, 108 TFW. via Rene Francillon

The 108th TFW Commander's personal jet, F-4E 68-0572 carried the name BENGALS on the gun fairing, and had the only tiger with white teeth and eyes. via Rene Francillon

FORT WORTH PHANTOM PHAREWELL was applied to F-4E 68-0389 for the 457 TFS/301 TFW F-4 close out. The unit flew Phantoms for 10 years – F-4Ds and later "E" models. Wally Van Winkle

F-4E 67-0395, G. T. BINNIS JET II, was decorated with the F-4's time-honored "Spook" mascot. This was another New Jersey ANG aircraft purchased by the Turkish Air Force. via Rene Francillon

Gear door art on 68-0389 is called PHANTOM OF THE 457th, with the "Spook" character playing a pipe organ that incorporates the barrels of the M-61A1 cannon. Walker

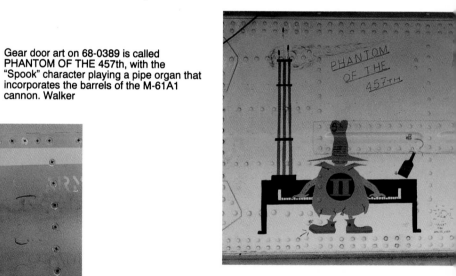

Art on F-4E 68-0533, 108 TFW, has the "Spook" on a desert island, with seagulls overhead. via Rene Francillon

SWAMP FOX, SILVER FOX is F-4E 68-0450 from the 457th TFS at Carswell. Walker

This warrior figure appears on the left splitter plate of F-4D 66-7583, of the 183rd TFG. Walker

DONT MESS WITH THE KID, well-weathered artwork on F-4C 64-0707 from the 171st FIS, 191st FIG, Michigan ANG. Paul Bigelow

AGNES is F-4C 64-0713. The name, and "My Dog" artwork, was applied while this Phantom served with the 123rd FIS, 142nd FIG, Oregon ANG at Portland. Wally Van Winkle

CITY OF CINCINNATI, OHIO is F-4D 66-7771 from the 906th TFG at Wright-Patterson AFB. It was common for 906th Phantoms to be named after Ohio cities, a practice which is continued on the Group's F-16s today. Wally Van Winkle

EXCALIBUR is F-4D 65-0659 from the 107th FIS, NYANG, at Niagra Falls. Gear door art applied especially for the jet's retirement flight to AMARC, including refueling stops on the way, bears the legend ARIZONA OR BUST and the date. The Niagra Falls Phantoms were replaced by F-16s. Wally Van Winkle

F-4D 66-7511, from the 507th TFG at Tinker AFB, was named SPIRIT OF OKC, with art depicting the skyline of Oklahoma City, for Mayor Ron Norick's orientation flight in the jet. 507 FG

Door art on F-4D 66-8816 FULL HOUSE, 704th TFS, 301 TFW. Jim Dunn

F-4D 66-8800 was almost certainly the last "D" operated by the U. S. Air Force – flown by the 3246th Test Wing at Eglin AFB. She was retired in 1992. Wally Van Winkle

"Spook"-shaped mission symbols on F-4G 69-0274 from the 52nd TFW. 23 Sept. 1991 was the day the aircraft was delivered to AMARC for storage. Walker

BULL'S EYE II is RF-4C 64-1083 from the 155th Reconnaissance Group based at Lincoln, Nebraska. Walker

PHANTOMS PHOREVER
1963 II 1992
END OF AN ERA

F-4G Wild Weasel 69-0244 of the 23rd TFS, 52nd TFW at Spangdahlem, Germany carries a charging black winged rhino on the nose – alluding to one of the Phantom's many nicknames. NIGHT STALKER has 27 "Spook" silhouettes on the left splitter plate, reflecting missions from Sheikh Isa during Desert Storm. Wally Van Winkle

RF-4C 66-0418 GIRLS JUST WANNA HAVE FUN is another 155th RG Phantom, most of which carry small artwork on the removable panel above the air conditioning intake scoop. Jim Meehan

RF-4C 65-0939 LADY DI also belongs to the 155th Reconnaissance Group, one of a handful of ANG units still flying the Phantom. Walker

Artwork representing the 152nd TRG's service in Desert Shield/Desert Storm, with 412 reconnaissance sorties out of Sheikh Isa AB in Bahrain, is seen here on RF-4C 65-0893. Jim Dunn

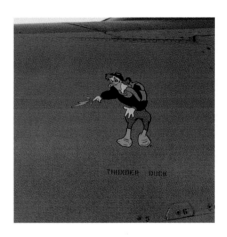

Similar art was carried on other RF-4C's including 64-1033, a 106th TRS Phantom from Alabama ANG at Birmingham that was operated by 152nd TRG crews from Reno, Nevada. Joe Bruch

RF-4C 65-0878 RAMBO was retired from the 155th RG on 14 January 1992. The 155th will soon transition from F-4s to KC-135 Stratotankers. Wally Van Winkle

CHARLIE, A.K.A. Charlie the Tuna, is seen on 155 RG RF-4C 65-0932. Wally Van Winkle

RECCE REBELS, BIRMINGHAM, RF-4C 65-0834 of the 106th TRS, 117 TRW was adorned with a caricature of a Confederate soldier aboard a Phantom. The jet was deployed to the Gulf as an attrition replacement for RF-4C 64-1044, lost 8 October 1990. David F. Brown

FREE SPIRIT, with mystical American Indian flavored artwork, is RF-4C 64-1062 from the 155th Reconnaissance Group at Lincoln, Nebraska. Bob Shane

RF-4C 65-0828, 155 RG, was named ELMER – apparently in reference to her crew chief. Wally Van Winkle

Bill the Cat riding on a missile appeared on RF-4C 64-1023, 155 RG, Nebraska ANG. Signatures were applied when the aircraft was sent to AMARC in the Spring of 1992. Wally Van Winkle

DOG BREATH is RF-4C 69-0920, from the 155th RG. Bob Shane

MISS PHOTO-GENIC is RF-4C 64-1066, 155 RG, 173 RS. The 155th has flown the tactical recce mission from 1964 with RF-84Fs, and RF-4Cs since 1972. Bob Shane

RF-4C 68-0551 of the 15th TRS, home-based at Taegu AB, South Korea, carried these NOGUN SHOGUN tail markings while taking part in Photo Finish '85 at McClellan AFB. The 15th TRS deactivated in 1991, handing over their jets to the RoKAF. Jim Dunn

CHAPTER 11

U-2R/TR-1A

TR-1A 80-1084, of the 9th Wing home based at Beale AFB, California, wears tail art in the form of a dragon's head. The TR-1A/U-2 recce aircraft has long been referred to by the unofficial name "Dragon Lady", which might explain why the mythical beasts often appear in their tail art. Jim Dunn

This artwork – featuring a dragon, crossed sabres, a planform view of the airplane, and a palm tree – was applied to TR-1A 80-1088 by Airman James R. Barden of the 9th SRW, using colored chalk sprayed with Scotchguard for protection. "OL CH" reportedly stands for Operating Location Camel Hump. Of note is the fact that the last two digits of the tail number appear to have been changed, a not uncommon practice for these jets. Jim Dunn

A desert Bart Simpson, with slingshot at the ready, was carried on the left side of TR-1A 80-1088's tail. TR-1As from Beale, Cyprus and the 17th RW at RAF Alconbury operated from Taif, Saudi Arabia under the 1704th Reconnaissance Squadron (Provisional) throughout the Gulf War. Jim Dunn

TR-1A 80-1074, 9th Wing, carries artwork depicting a dog sniffing out a Scud missle – indicative of the type's Scud-hunting duties out of Taif. N. Donald

An angry green-eyed bee armed with a camera is worn by TR-1A 80-1094 of the 9th Wing. TR-1A's still carry photographic recce equipment, as well as airborne synthetic aperture radar and signal intelligence gathering devices. Jim Dunn

TR-1A 80-1098 belongs to the 9th Wing, 99th Reconnaissance Squadron. Jim Dunn

Tail art on TR-IA 80-0199 from the 9th W shows "Spaceman Spiff" gritting his teeth and snapping photos with a 35mm camera. The TR-1As were recently redesignated as U-2Rs. L. N. Paul

CHAPTER 12
F-105 THUNDERCHIEF

F-105D 62-4347 was named STAR DUST 6 while serving with the 466th TFS, 419th TFW, AFRES. Displaying the wraparound SEA paint scheme to good advantage, she remains in perpetual flight on a pole at Hill AFB, Utah – a kinder fate than befell most of the Thuds that survived to retirement. Paul Bigelow

KILLER ACE was 149th TFS, 192nd TFG F-105F 62-4418. She belonged to the Kansas ANG before going to Virginia. Jim Meehan

NO GUTS NO GLORY, art by TSgt "Beetle" Bailey, appeared on F-105D 62-4353 while serving with the Virginia ANG; and went with the Thud to the 301st TFW in Texas when the 192nd transitioned to A-7Ds. The same jet was named "Billie Fern" with the 355th TFW in Southeast Asia. Jim Meehan

F-105D 61-0145 from the 192nd TFG was named MY HONEYPOT in 1979. The name was a version of "Honeypot II" – originally carried on MiG killer 61-0159 with the 355th TFW, which ended up assigned to the Virginia ANG as "Have Gun Will Travel." The art on 61-0145 was deemed to be too suggestive and was removed, leaving only the rainbow. Jim Meehan

Virginia ANG F-105D 61-0170 THUNDER AX, an ex-23rd TFW Thud, earned her name by taking out several trees and a utility pole with one wing on a North Carolina bombing range. Jim Meehan

F-105D 61-0159 HAVE GUN WILL TRAVEL was one of an elite few Thud MiG killers. The kill was made while serving with the 355th TFW in the lage 1960s, though no other details are known. The names "Honeypot II" and "Have Gun Will Travel" were applies to the jet while in 355th service, the latter remaining throughout her stint with the Virginia ANG. This was the first Thud to reach 4,000 hours. Jim Meehan

Another Virginia ANG 192 TFG F-105D (62-4384), RED RIVER RAIDER saw action in Southeast Asia with the 355th TFW at Takhli RTAB and presumably became quite familiar with the Red River area. Jim Meehan

F-105D 59-1739 was named QUEEN OF THE FLEET during her tenure with the Virginia Air Guard's 192nd TFG. The same aircraft was known as "Rum Runner" while with the 388th TFW in 1967. Jim Meehan

HANOI EXPRESS – F-105D 59-1743 of the Virginia ANG – flew with the 388th TFW in 1967 as "Darn Dago", and became the 388th CO's mount "Arkansas Traveller" in '68. As "Lead Zeppelin" she fought with the 355th TFW at Takhli in 1970. Jim Meehan

THE BOSS, F-105D 61-0050, was placed on a column at the entrance to the Guard area of Byrd Field in Richmond when her flying days with the 192nd TFG ended. Jim Meehan

CHAPTER 13
US NAVY/MARINES

Though any artwork was ordered removed from U.S. Navy aircraft before their return home from the Gulf, this example survived – covered with paper and sprayed gray for camouflage. When E-2C 161552 MISS B. HAVIN of VAW-124 returned home to NAS Norfolk, her nose art was then unveiled. David F. Brown

E-2C 160416, of VAW-78 Fighting Escargots, carries mission markings from the war on drugs – what appears to be a Gulfstream business jet and 5 single-engine light planes stencilled on the port side. Hawkeyes on occasion provide radar coverage for anti-smuggling operations in and near U.S. territory. Walker

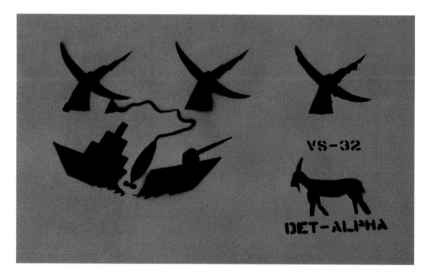

A few S-3 Viking squadrons, left without a primary mission due to the lack of an Iraqi submarine threat, carried out strikes on surface targets. This S-3B, 159765, of VS-32 Maulers destroyed three radar sites and a Khuk class gunboat. The boat was sunk in a most unusual way, utilizing three Mk-82 500lb bombs and (by mistake) a buddy refueling pod. The goat represents VS-32's detachment at Souda Bay on the island of Crete. David F. Brown

F-14A 162603 of VF-I Wolfpack , operating off the U.S.S. Ranger scored the only F-14 air-to-air kill of the Gulf War. Lt. Stuart Broce, pilot, and Cdr Ron McElraft, RIO, downed an Iraqi Mi-8 "Hip" helicopter with an AIM-9 Sidewinder on 6 February, 1991. David F. Brown

This F-14A, the CAG bird for VF-32 Swordsmen , carries two MiG-23 silhouettes, representing the two Libyan MiGs downed by VF-32 Tomcats 159437 (callsign GYPSY 207) and 159610 (GYPSY 202) while flying CAP off the USS John F. Kennedy on 4 January 1989. L. N. Paul

A-6E 161669 of VMA(AW)-224, home based at MCAS Cherry Point, North Carolina, had this tiger applied to the right side of the nose radome when photographed in October 1992. Jim Dunn

SPANKY EA-6B 163524 belongs to VAQ-131 Lancers , embarked aboard U.S.S. Ranger during the Gulf War. Walker

F/A-18A 162468, of VMFA-314 Black Knights, completed 67 missions from Sheikh Isa AB, Bahrain, with stencilled kill markings representing several types of targets; Scud launcher, APC, tank, anti-aircraft gun and even a small ship. David F. Brown

F/A-18C 163502 carries a MiG-21 silhouette on either side of the nose. VFA-81 Hornets scored the Navy's only air-to-air fixed-wing kills of the war. Walker

Lieutenant Nick "Mongo" Mongillo shot down an Iraqi F-7A (Chinese-built version of the MiG-21) while at the controls of VFA-81 Sunliners F/A-18C 163502 on 17 January 1991. Four Navy Hornets were inbound to a ground target when two F-7As engaged a pair of them. Lt. Mongillo and Lt. Cdr Ed Fox (in F/A-18C 163508) each bagged one MiG using AIM-9 Sidewinders, and then proceeded to strike the ground target as planned. Walker

Mission markings in the form of lightning bolts on EA-6B 160435 of VMAQ-2. Twelve Prowlers, the U.S. Marine Corps' only dedicated electronic warfare aircraft, operated out of Sheikh Isa during Desert Storm. Walker

111

The Corsair II seemed fated to fade quietly out of service with the U.S. Navy, but instead went out in a blaze of glory when the last two squadrons to fly the A-7 (VA-46 and VA-72) were deployed aboard the U.S.S. John F. Kennedy at the beginning of Desert Shield. This A-7E, 160713 was flown to AMARC on 10 June 1991 for storage after decommissioning of VA-46 Clansmen on 23 May 1991. In deferrence to her war record the Spraylat was carefully applied around her scoreboard which features a variety of mission symbols, including General Purpose iron bombs, Rockeyes and HARMs. Walker

A-7E 160552 of VA-72 Bluehawks was painted in this special desert camouflage prior to leaving the deck of the U.S.S. John F. Kennedy for the last time. The aircraft flew 31 combat missions in the standard overall gray scheme and received the paint job on the cruise home to NAS Cecil Field, Florida. M. D. Swann via Paul Bigelow

F-4S 155805 wears a very non-standard paint scheme, applied for the type's retirement from VMFA-212 Lancers in 1988. Wally Van Winkle

Several AV-8B Harriers of Marine Attack Squadron VMA-231 Aces carried the inscription "Free Kuwait" in Arabic beside their ace-of-spades unit markings. Seen here, 163665 is a 59-mission combat veteran. Walker

The U.S. Navy is currently expending about four QF-4 unmanned target drones per year. QF-4N 152269, of the Naval Air Warfare Center, is utilized mainly for testing purposes and usually is flown in the traditional manner by a pilot onboard the aircraft. As a result, 152269 has enjoyed a rather lengthy life as a QF-4. The U.S. Air Force will convert many of its excess F-4Es and F-4Gs into target aircraft when the QF-106 drone program is completed. Jim Dunn.

SAGEBURNER, F4H-1F (F-4A) 145307, displays the low streamlined canopy and small pointed nose radome particular to the first 18 Phantoms. The 8th Phantom built, SAGEBURNER set a new world speed record for low level flight on 28 August 1961 – 902.769 mph at an altitude not exceeding 328 ft (l00m). Within a month, another Phantom (142260, "Skyburner") set an absolute speed record of 1,606.3 mph. SAGEBURNER now belongs to the National Air and Space Museum and is kept in storage at Silver Hill, Maryland. via Rene Francillon

U.S. Marine Reserve Squadron VMFA-321 "Hell's Angels" applied this high-visibility scheme – similar to that used by the unit in the colorful 1970s – to F-4S 153904 to commemorate the retirement of their Phantoms, in preparation for F/A-18A Hornets. via Rene Francillon

113

A-4F 154172, one of several stripped-down Skyhawks operated in the adversary role by VF-43 Challengers, wears the name BULLET fitting for such a small and strikingly agile jet. Jim Meehan

Another VS-32 S-3B, 159751 WORLD FAMOUS MAULERS carried this pin-up, and the unit's full designation: "32nd Torpedo Attack Squadron.' David F. Brown

CUJO is another A-4F, 154211, belonging to VF-43 at NAS Oceana. The elderly Skyhawk continues to perform adversary duties admirably alongside newer and more expensive aircraft like the F-16N. Jim Meehan

EYES OF THE STORM appeared briefly on a S-3B Viking. David F. Brown

Being the biggest, heaviest jet on the Navy's aircraft carriers earned the Douglas A-3 Skywarrior the derogatory nickname "Whale", that as time passed became a term of endearment. The natural choice for naming one's A-3, therefore, became KILLER WHALE. One of the last whales flying, EA-3B 146454 of VQ-2 Batmen even sports an angry shark mouth. Paul Bigelow

This KILLER WHALES EA-3B, 144852 of VQ-2, was retired in late 1990 and is now stored at the Aerospace Maintenance And Regeneration Center in Tucson, AZ. Bob Shane

EKA-3B 142659 was named KILLER WHALE while serving with VAW-13 in September, 1968. Seen here at NAS Cubi Point, she also carried a small rendering of cartoon character Andy Capp on the nose radome. Jim Meehan

EKA-3B 142252 was stationed aboard the USS Constellation with VAH-I0 Vikings when photographed in 1968. The black sword carried on both sides of the fuselage was apparently a unit marking, though it is believed that this "bloodied" version was a more individualized bit of artwork. Jim Meehan

Oceanographic Development Squadron Eight (VXN-8) operates a colorful fleet of Lockheed P-3 Orions. RP-3A 150500, ARCTIC FOX, was assigned to "Project Birdseye" — a long term study of the polar ice fields. Wearing an attractive red and white paint scheme for conspicuity in the snowy polar regions, ARCTIC FOX is seen in May 1981 at VXN-8's home station, NAS Patuxent River, Maryland. This aircraft was retired on 11 July 1991, with a total of 20,200 flight hours, to be replaced by RP-3D 184587. L.N. Paul

UP-3A 150528, a P-3A with her ASW gear removed, was used by VXN-8 as a utility support aircraft. For a time the aircraft remained in plain grey and white trim, with nose art in the form of Snoopy the WWI flying ace. L.N. Paul

UP-3A 150528 eventually received the high-vis VXN-8 paint job and the name LOON, along with art inspired by the comic strip "Shoe." Wally Van Winkle

Seen in retirement: UP-3A 150527, another VXN-8 utility bird, carried the ever-popular Warner Brothers cartoon character TASMA-NIAN DEVIL. Walker

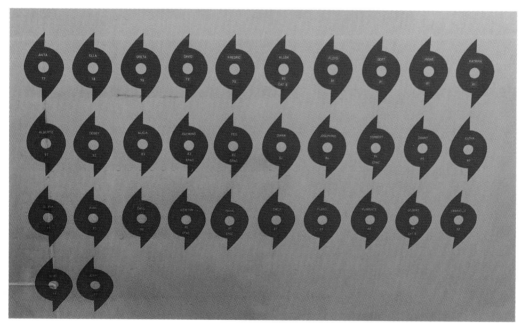

The National Oceanic and Atmospheric Administration operates a pair of weather reconnaissance WP-3D Orions out of Miami, which carry their own variety of mission markings. Built on the basic P-3C airframe/engine combination, the WP-3Ds monitor and track developing hurricanes from the inside, using radars and airflow sensors as well as the standard Mk.1 eyeball. At the beginning of the 1990 hurricane season, N43RF-assigned BuNo 159875 during construction – proudly displayed "kills" dating from Anita in 1977 to Hugo and Jerry in 1989. Walker

EP-3E 157320, EVELYN of VQ-2, carries 21 mission symbols in the shape of active radar sets. VQ-2 EP-3E "Aries" electronic surveillance aircraft were based at Bahrain (and possibly in Turkey) during Desert Storm – but 157320, newly converted from a P-3C, wasn't delivered to the unit until the spring of 1991. The mission marks refer to her crew's service in the Gulf aboard the aging EP-3E she replaced. Paul Bigelow

This small artwork is also found on EP-3E 157320. Paul Bigelow

EP-3E 157320 EVELYN, on the go at RAF Fairford, displays the large underfuselage radome, and dorsal and ventral canoe fairings that house extremely sophisticated surveillance equipment. EVELYN was the first new EP-3E "Aries II" variant, converted to replace the tired original EP-3Es (themselves modified P-3As). Paul Bigelow

Two P-3Cs from VP-91 "Stingers", a Naval Reserve unit based at NAS Moffett Field, California, flew surveillance and reconnaissance missions in the Persian Gulf during Desert Storm. Two Iraqi ship silhouettes are carried on 163295. Jim Dunn

An unusual place to find a sharkmouth is the Navy's Basic Jet trainer, the T-2 Buckeye, such as "319." L.N. Paul

AH-1J Sea Cobra 157785 of Marine Reserve Squadron HMA-773 carried the name SCARFACE along with a cobra silhouette. Despite the relative age of the AH-1J (first deliveries in 1969) two squadrons of "J" model Sea Cobras deployed to the Mid East for Operation Desert Storm. Walker

This U.S. Navy SH-2F Sea Sprite helicopter, 151321, ZULU INVADER belongs to HSL-32 Tridents. Jim Meehan

CH-46E Sea Knight 157656, THE BULLET, belongs to HMM-264. Jim Meehan

SH-2F 162576 wears kill markings – a gunboat and an oil platform – from tanker escort operations in the Persian Gulf in the late 1980s, and the insignia of HSL-35 Det. 7 "Daredevils." Wally Van Winkle

Also from HSL-32, FIFI SH-2F 161642 wears mission markings from ops associated with the Operation El Dorado Canyon strike against Libya in 1986. White submarine silhouettes indicate U.S. or "friendly" subs located, and red silhouettes stand for Russian subs located. Jim Meehan

SH-2F 150140 LOST BOYS belongs to Det.5 of HSL-35 Magicians, shore-based at NAS North Island. Jim Dunn

CHAPTER 14
C-130 HERCULES

C-130E 63-7849 assigned to the 23rd Wing wears an enlarged version of the Flying Tiger sharkmouth carried on their A 10 Warthogs. The 23rd is authorized to put sharkmouths on any aircraft they fly. Jim Meehan

The new 23rd Wing C-130 sharkmouths appear especially menacing when viewed from the front, as on this example, C-130E 63-9810, photographed at Airlift Rodeo 92. Jim Dunn

From the 164th TAG, Tennessee ANG, – the last USAF unit to operate the C-130A – 57-0463 carries the name and Petty Girl artwork of the famous MEMPHIS BELLE. Margaret Polk, the "Memphis Belle" who Captain Bob Morgan named his B-17 after during the early days of U.S. involvment in WWII, is memorialized in the artwork. The 164th TAG C-130As gave way to C-141's in 1991-92. Bob Shane

This 314 TAW C-130E, 63-7776, ARKANSAS DREAMIN carries a nice piece of artwork and a very impressive mission tally for Operation Desert Shield and the postwar Kurdish relief effort, Operation Provide Comfort. This is a testament to the reliability of the C-130 and the hard work of the crew. Bob Shane

A close-up view of the art on ARKANSAS DREAMIN. Two of the most prevalent themes of nose art throughout the years remain girls and home. Bob Shane

When away from Little Rock AFB, crewman Sgt John Briggs likes to dress up the aircraft, in this case CHRISTINE, 314 TAW C-130E 64-0557, with a bit of temporary nose art. Named for Stephen King's 1958 Plymouth Fury title character, at times CHRISTINE seems to have a mind of her own – equipment thought to be broken suddenly working again, etc. The chalk is easily removed when it's time to go home. Walker

Lightning bolts serve as mission symbols on EC-130H 73-1581, a Compass Call radio jammer from the 41st ECS at Davis Monthan AFB. Compass Call aircraft were used to jam Iraqi communications during Desert Storm and may have used their "spoofing" ability to broadcast misleading orders over the enemy communication network. Walker

C-130H 78-0813 from the 137th AW, Oklahoma ANG, was decorated with this OKIE GUARD DOG chalk art for an airshow appearance in Spring of 1992. Walker

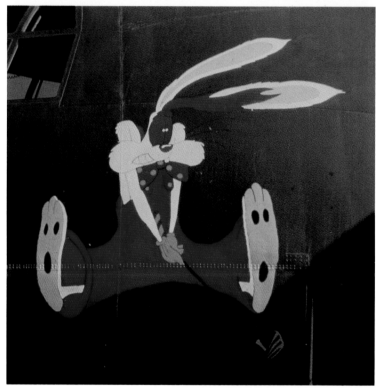

C-130E 68-10935 from the 435th TAW, 37th TAS at Rhein-Main AB, Germany, received Gulf War nose art in the form of a golfing Roger Rabbit; who is stunned by the size of the sand trap he's in.
USAF/MSgt Jose Lopez

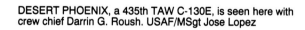

DESERT PHOENIX, a 435th TAW C-130E, is seen here with crew chief Darrin G. Roush. USAF/MSgt Jose Lopez

C-130E 69-6583 was given some pretty elaborate artwork and the name SAND SURFER by an artist who signed his (or her) name as "JAZ." USAF/MSgt Jose Lopez

PAYBACK TIME was C-130H 64-18240 from the 435 TAW. USAF/MSgt Jose Lopez

Artwork on C-130E 70-1274, 435 TAW, consists of a bulldog wearing a "U.S.A." armband and messily devouring the word "Iraq." USAF/MSgt Jose Lopez

Teenage Mutant Ninja Turtles-inspired artwork, DONATELLO, DESERT NINJA was found on C-130E 69-6582 from the 435 TAW. USAF/MSgt Jose Lopez

SAND SHARK is another example of C-130 Desert Shield nose art. USAF/MSgt Jose Lopez

The newest USAF Gunship, the prototype AC-130U (87-0128) carries on the tradition of "Spectre" nose art, though the usual dark gray or black paint scheme has been abandoned for European One camouflage - while airlifter C-130s are being painted gray. The aircraft is assigned to the 6512th Test Squadron at Edwards AFB. Jim Dunn

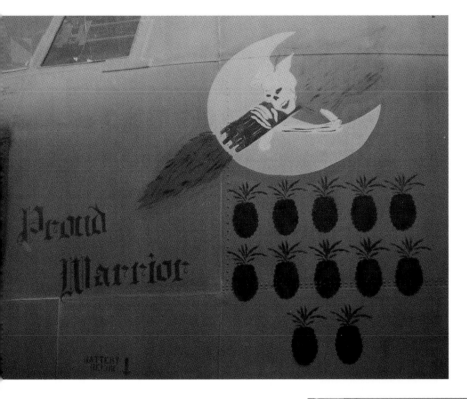

Veteran AC-130A 54-1630 AZRAEL, ANGEL OF DEATH, 919th SOG, with Gulf War mission marks and a faceless "Spectre." Wally Van Winkle

PROUD WARRIOR, 919 SOG AC-130A 55-0046, carries a dozen pineapple mission symbols that represent sorties flown in Operation Just Cause, the 1989 invasion of Panama. David F. Brown

AC-130A 55-0014, from the 711th Special Operations Squadron, 919th Special Operations Group home based at Duke Field, Florida, JAWS OF DEATH carries 23 mission symbols earned while taking part in Operation Proven Force — striking from Turkey during the Gulf War against targets in northern Iraq where Saudi-based aircraft would be hard-pressed to reach. David F. Brown

CITY OF JACKSONVILLE is C-130E 63-7850 of the 314 Airlift Wing. Jacksonville, Arkansas is located near Little Rock AFB, about where the star is on the state map. Jim Dunn

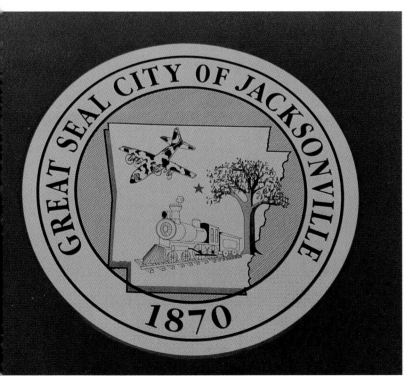

AC-130H 69-6575, a 16th Special Operations Squadron Spectre gunship, displays mission symbols or kills in the form of 5 armored vehicles. Wally Van Winkle

MC-130E Mod 90 64-0565 is utilized by the 8th Special Operations Squadron at Hurlburt Field, Florida, as a testbed for equipment to be used on other Combat Talon MC-130s. THE GUTS TO TRY, with a phoenix logo, is carried on the right side; and a muscular bird armed with sword and lighting is on the left. Wally Van Winkle

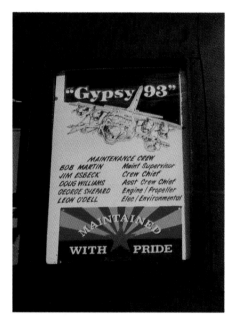

C-130A 56-0493 CITY OF TUCSON was operated by the 162nd TFG, Arizona ANG, as a hack for many years. The 162nd now has a C-130H support aircraft and CITY OF TUCSON is on static display at Davis-Monthan AFB. The placard placed in the side window lists the bird's maintenance crew, call sign "Gypsy 93", and depicts her flying with an AZ ANG F-16 and A-7. Wally Van Winkle

CHAPTER 15
F-117A STEALTH FIGHTER

The Lockheed F-117A has led military aviation into the age of low observable "Stealth" technology, proving that such an aircraft can be produced and employed effectively in combat. F-117As from the 37th TFW undertook more than 1,200 strike sorties against heavily defended targets during the Gulf War, scoring 1,600 direct hits without losing any aircraft or suffering any damage. This 415 TFS F-117A, 84-0826, went to war – and flew 29 combat missions – with Donald Duck artwork and the name NACHTFALKE –"Night Hawk" in German – painted on the inside of the weapons bay door. David F. Brown, and 37 FW

The likeness of actress Delta Burke was carried on DELTA DAWN, F-117A 81-0794, 415 TFS. She flew 35 Gulf War sorties. 237 FW

AFFECTIONATELY CHRISTINE is F-117A 88-0843 from the 415th TFS, 37th TFW. According to official 37th FW documents, -843 flew 33 Desert Storm missions. 37 FW

F-117A 86-0839, from the 415th TFS "Nightstalkers", was MIDNIGHT REAPER, which undertook 39 missions from the brand new facility at Khamis Mushait in Southern Saudi Arabia. 37 FW

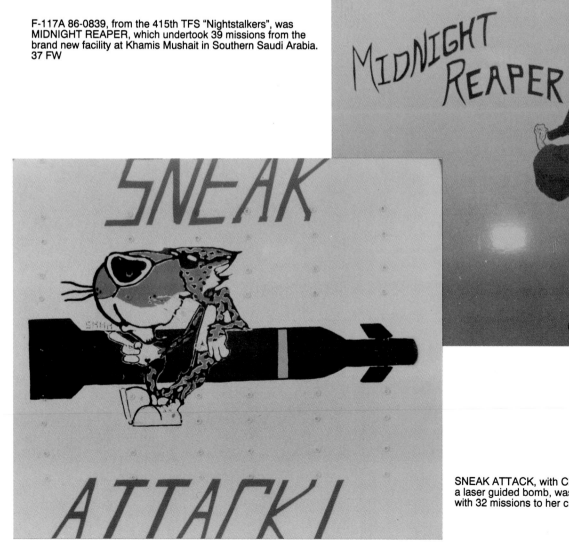

SNEAK ATTACK, with Chester Cheetah casually leaning against a laser guided bomb, was found on 415th TFS F-117A 86-0821 with 32 missions to her credit. 37 FW

The weapons bay art on F-117A 84-0825, MAD MAX, of the 415 TFS, illustrates the 37th TFW's deployment to Saudi Arabia. The orders were received at Tonopah Test Range at 1400 hours on 17 August 1990 and twenty-one 415th TFS aircraft left for a different desert on 19 August. After stopping overnight at Langley AFB, VA, the F-117As arrived in Saudi on 21 Aug (with the 416th TFS to follow) and on 26 Aug the Black Jet assumed alert duty for the first time. 37 FW

The name MAD MAX was also applied to the inside of the nosewheel door on Lt. Col. Ralph Getchell's F-117A. This aircraft flew a total of 33 combat sorties. Jim Meehan

LONE WOLF was F-117A 85-0816, 415 TFS, a veteran of 39 combat sorties. 37 FW

Bart Simpson, a very popular Gulf War art subject, even found his way into the Stealth Fighter's weapons bay. Bart accompanied THE OVERACHIEVER, F-117A 85-0818, 415 TFS, on 38 missions from Khamis Mushait. 37 FW

This art was applied to F-117A 84-0812, the 415th TFS "Frequent Flyer" with squadron-high total of 42 sorties. 37 FW

DOUBLE DOWN is F-117A 84-0811, 415 TFS, 37 TFW. Until recently relocating to Holloman AFB, New Mexico, and becoming the 49th FW; Team Stealth was home-based at Tonopah Test Range in Nevada. The artwork alludes to the state's gambling heritage. This Black Jet flew 33 Desert Storm missions. 37 FW

THE CHICKENHAWK, F-117A 83-0807, from the 415 TFS, completed 14 sorties as part of the 37th Tactical Fighter Wing Provisional at Khamis Mushait. 37 FW

F-117A 83-0803 from the 415 TFS, was named THOR at the time of the Gulf War and is credited with 37 combat missions. 37 FW

F-117A 85-0819 was RAVEN BEAUTY, a 30-mission 416th TFS Black Jet. Throughout the Gulf War, the 37th TFW(P) launched two or three waves per night depending on the distance to the targets. 37 FW

130

SOMETHING WICKED was carried on F-117A 82-0806, 415 TFS, 37 TFW. From the time the first Desert Storm sorties launched at 0022 hours local time on 17 January, until the attacks were stopped on the night of 27 February, -806 flew 39 missions. 37 FW

PERPETRATOR, F-117A 82-0801 of the 415th TFS, is a 38 mission combat veteran. 237 FW

F-117A 81-0798, a 415th TFS Black Jet with 34 missions to her credit, was named ACES AND EIGHTS. Interestingly the card suit of Spades is represented by planform silhouettes of the aircraft. 37 FW

FATAL ATTRACTION, F-117A 81-0796 from the 415th TFS, completed 29 nocturnal attack missions against "high-value" Iraqi targets. 37 FW

WILEY E. COYOTE'S TRITONAL EXPRESS, was F-117A 81-0793, 415 TFS. LGBs like the one pictured here were the Stealth Fighter's weapon of choice in the Gulf; including GBU-10 Paveway, GBU-12 Paveway II, and GBU-27 Paveway III – with shortened nose and clipped fins to fit inside the F-117A's weapons bay. 33 missions are credited to -793. 37 FW

F-117A 80-0791, LAZY ACE, with art depicting a "Stealth Biplane" complete with subdued national insignia and tail number, completed 33 Gulf War sorties. 37 FW

DEADLY JESTER appeared on the center-hinged weapons bay door of F-117A 80-0790 from the 415th TFS. Upon returning from a sortie against the chemical warfare facility at Samarra on 9 February, this jet blew a nose wheel tire on landing. Pieces of the tire damaged the underside of the aircraft and three air data probes. DEADLY JESTER completed 30 missions. 37 FW

Displaying the eerie head-on aspect of the Black Jet that may have inspired someone in the media to create the "Wobbly Goblin" monniker, BLACK MAGIC was found on F-117A 80-0789, a 31 mission 415th TFS aircraft. 37 FW

WAR PIG was F-117A 80-0786; the lowest-serialled, and presumably the oldest, Stealth Fighter deployed to Saudi. This 416th TFS, 37th TFW jet completed 24 combat sorties. 37 FW

F-117A 81-0797 SPELL BOUND from the 416th TFS Ghost Riders, 37th TFW, flew 8 Desert Storm sorties. 37 FW

AVENGING ANGEL, F-117A 85-0829 from the 416th TFS, with a total of 23 combat sorties. 37 FW

Door art on 416 TFS F-117A 82-0799 MIDNIGHT RIDER depicts a character similar to the "Silver Surfer" Marvel Comics superhero, flying through space on a F-117 shaped object. This aircraft is credited with 21 combat missions. 237 FW

BLACK MAGIC appeared on F-117A 82-0802 of the 416th TFS, a veteran of 19 Desert Storm sorties. The elements of magic and creatures of the night are understandably prevalent in F-117 artwork. 37 FW

Probably the most frequently seen example of F-117A weapons bay door art is THE TOXIC AVENGER, 85-0813, a 35-mission 416th TFS jet. This was the personal mount of 37th TFW Commander Col. Alton C. Whitley during the Gulf War. 37 FW

The art on 416 TFS F-117A 82-0803 features "Beetlejuice", the motion picture and television "Ghost with the most", riding a LGB right through the door. UNEXPECTED GUEST participated in 33 strikes on Iraqi targets. 37 FW

FINAL VERDICT, F-117A 85-0814, 416th TFS, 34 missions. 37 FW

DARK ANGEL, F-117A 84-0810 from the 416th TFS, flew 26 Desert Storm missions. 37 FW

F-117A 85-0817 SHABA, from the 416th TFS, undertook 18 combat sorties. 37 FW

BLACK DEVIL was F-117A 85-0833 from the 416th TFS, which completed 30 sorties. 237 FW

F-117A 85-0830 from the 416th TFS was named BLACK ASSASSIN, and flew 31 missions over Iraq. The average mission lasted 5 1/2 hours, with up to 45 minutes in enemy airspace. The Black Jet was the only aircraft allowed to overfly downtown Baghdad, which was defended by an estimated 3000 anti-aircraft guns and over 50 SAM sites. 37 FW, Walker

F-117A 85-0834, NECROMANCER of the 416th TFS, flew 34 missions. 37 FW

F-117A 85-0832, 416TFS, with 30 combat sorties, was named ONCE BITTEN and carried this artwork on the weapons bay door. In addition to taking part in the November 1991 Imminent Thunder joint exercise, the 37th TFW(later TFWP) conducted a trio of limited operational readiness exercises – titled Sneaky Sultan I, II, and III – in October, November, and December. 37 FW

THE DRAGON, F-117A 85-0835 from the 416th TFS, wore the insignia of the "Dragon Test Team" – Det 1 of the 57th Fighter Weapons Wing at Nellis AFB. 37 FW

F-117A 88-0841, 416 TFS, carried this artwork on 18 combat sorties from Khamis Mushait. The 37th TFW's new emblem – which added a black Nighthawk to the old "Defender of the Crossroads" insignia used during the wing's years of flying F-4's out of George AFB – is represented on MYSTIC WARRIOR's shield. 37 FW

BLACK WIDOW is F-117A, 86-0840, a 32 mission 416th TFS Black Jet. The art is quite similar to that on 81-0796 from the 415th. 37th FW

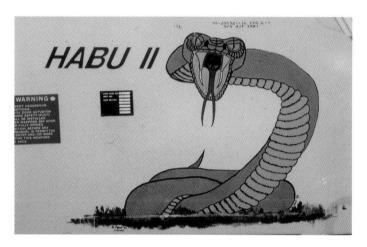

HABU II, on F-117A 86-0837, from the 416th TFS, draws inspiration from another breakthrough aircraft from Lockheed – the SR-71, nicknamed "Habu" after a poisonous viper found in parts of Asia. The original version of this artwork included an F-117A behind the snake, visible between its coiled body and head. HABU II flew 31 Desert Storm sorties. 37th FW

Art on F-117A, 86-0838, MAGIC HAMMER features a female warrior equipped with a golden hammer and shield emblazoned with the insignia of the 416th TFS. This aircraft is credited with 36 combat missions. 37th FW

CHRISTINE door art on F-117A 85-0836 depicts a sinister red Stealth Fighter with landing lights ablaze. This 416th Ghost Riders jet completed 39 combat sorties in the Gulf. 37 FW

IT'S HAMMERTIME, a phrase made popular by rap star Hammer, was applied to F-117A 88-0842 from the 416th TFS. This jet flew 33 Gulf War combat missions. 37 FW